# MIDLAND RED COACHES

### DAVID HARVEY

AMBERLEY

# Acknowledgments

The author is grateful to the many photographers acknowledged in the text who have contributed to this volume. Some of the photographs are more than ninety years old and are impossible to trace. Thanks are also due to the late Geoff Atkins, Roy Marshall, Les Mason and Peter Yeomans, who all printed photographs for me many years ago and generously gave permission for me to use their material. Where the photographer is not known, the photographs are credited to my own collection. Special thanks are due to my wife Diana for her splendid proof reading. The book would not have been possible without the continued encouragement given by Louis Archard and Connor Stait at Amberley Publishing.

First published 2020

Amberley Publishing
The Hill, Stroud
Gloucestershire, GL5 4EP

www.amberley-books.com

Copyright © David Harvey, 2020

The right of David Harvey to be identified as the Author
of this work has been asserted in accordance with the
Copyrights, Designs and Patents Act 1988.

British Library Cataloguing in Publication Data.
A catalogue record for this book is available from the British Library.

ISBN 978 1 4456 6798 0 (print)
ISBN 978 1 4456 6799 7 (ebook)

Typeset in 9pt on 12pt Sabon.
Origination by Amberley Publishing.
Printed in the UK.

# Contents

# Introduction

The problem with compiling a book about coaches is that many of the locations are difficult to identify, especially when the coach is on a tour. If there is no identifying feature, nor building that is still extant into the twenty-first century and the photographer did not note the location, it can be almost impossible to identify where the photograph was taken. This is especially true of the pre-1930 vehicles, where frequently an overloaded charabanc is parked in front of a hotel or hostelry, when the picture was taken, to show who was on the office or works outing in the 'roaring twenties'. Trilby hats for the men and the cloche hats for the women frequently added to the stern, unsmiling faces of the passengers and their formal poses. They were probably having a lovely time on the day trip or excursion with the Midland Red, but sometimes they look really glum!

The Second World War put an end to coaching and trips to the seaside and many coaches were either impressed by the War Department, converted to buses or used to transport troops. By the summer of 1946, restricted day excursions resumed. With the post-war fuel restrictions on private cars, coach travel became a real alternative to the rundown railways, and when Midland Red coach excursions for between seven and twelve days began to expand, it became necessary to have an influx of the newly developed BMMO underfloor engined chassis bodied as luxury coaches. Between 1948 and 1954, no less than 152 new coaches put Midland Red at the forefront of British coaching activity, enabling Midland Red's reputation to become further enhanced with this new fleet of coaches. This was the zenith of Midland Red's coaching interests, which was reflected in the company advertisements that stated they were 'the Friendly Midland Red'.

The opening of the first section of the M1 Motorway, on 2 November 1959, was another milestone in the coaching activities of Midland Red. The M1 would eventually go from London to Leeds, but the initial section was from Junction 18 at Crick near Rugby to Junction 5 at Watford. And for the new service a batch of seventy-four new coaches were constructed. There were several sub-groups within the class, but the most famous must have had the fastest toilets on the road, as they had that facility at the rear of the coach, were turbo-charged and could reach speeds well in excess of 85 mph. The facilities on board enabled the coaches to leave either Birmingham or Coventry and go non-stop to Victoria coach station in the capital. The performance of these coaches became the stuff of legend, to the extent that Corgi made a model of the CM5T motorway express coaches. The success of these coaches, however, resulted in Midland Red being hoist by their own petard. The coming of the new 'box' dimensions in 1961 enabled 36-foot-long vehicles, with increased carrying capacity, to ply their trade, which meant that the original Midland Red motorway coaches were at a disadvantage. In 1962, BMMO rectified this by producing the CM6T prototype, which was an extended version of the pioneers and similarly based on the framework of their own new 'box' dimensions buses; in 1965 and 1966 twenty-nine production vehicles were placed into service. From 1965, the standard coach chassis became the Leyland Leopard and it was only in 1981 that a solitary Leyland Tiger chassis was purchased.

# An Overall Summary of Midland Red Coaching

As well as being one of the largest bus operators in the United Kingdom, the Birmingham & Midland Motor Omnibus Company also operated a large number of coaches, starting with charabancs (coaches with benches), in 1914, through to heavyweight underfloor-engined luxury coaches in the early 1980s. From the earliest days just before the First World War, the Birmingham & Midland Motor Omnibus Company, as well as operating an increasing large number of buses for stage carriage operation to cover bus services over a rapidly expanding geographical area, began running coach excursions and express bus services not just to seaside resorts, but to London and other major cities.

Throughout the pre-war years, the company expanded its coach tours. Excursions, particularly to the South West and North Wales, as well as long-distance stage carriage services radiated from the Birmingham area as far as Gloucester, Hereford, Shrewsbury, Leicester and Northampton. The early Tilling-Stevens charabancs gave way to more sophisticated, albeit somewhat archaic-looking, normal-control touring coaches. These were built by the company itself as the SOS marque at Carlyle Road Works – a policy that would continue until 1966 when the final 'homemade' BMMO motorway coaches entered service.

At the beginning of the 1930s, the somewhat idiosyncratic-looking SOS models, such as the RR-type, had come to prominence and, despite their weird-looking tiny offset driver's cabs, were quite powerful with engine sizes about the same as contemporary commercially manufactured coach chassis. But where they stood out was their lightweight construction, which enabled them to have a sparkling turn of speed and an economical rate of fuel consumption. These interwar half-cab coaches required something more modern and, by the middle of the 1930s, the company began to produce full-fronted coaches with well-styled, thoroughly up-to-date bodies, whose appearance attracted more and more customers to Midland Red. The SOS SLRs and ONCs were to transform Midland Red's coaching image just before the outbreak of war and despite the privations of the hostilities, these coaches soldiered on until the early and mid-1950s and still looked modern and contemporary.

Vehicle development during the war was restricted to the rebuilding of the four experimental rear-engined single-deckers, one of which was a coach registered CHA 1, into prototype underfloor-engined buses. Once these had been introduced as production buses in the S6 and S8 classes, they soon spawned the first fleet of post-war coaches, also with underfloor engines. In 1948 and 1949, forty-five C1 coaches were introduced, along with twelve similar C2 touring coaches, which suddenly placed Midland Red at the forefront of post-war coaching activities. A further sixty-three of the larger C3 coaches, built to the new 30-foot length and 8-foot width, along with twelve C4 touring heavyweight coaches, added further stock to the coach fleet and enabled Midland Red to further expand its coaching business.

In 1959, the company saw the opening of the initial section of the M1 as a golden opportunity to provide both a very fast service to London and to gain a lot of prestige and publicity for the name Midland Red. The result was the BMMO C5 family, which, with all its variations of being turbocharged, having four or five-speed gearboxes and with or without toilets, comprised some seventy-four units plus the prototype. Those employed on the express motorway service were, as stated above, too popular with passengers. Initially too fast but too small, they were capable of overtaking all but the fastest production British saloon and sports cars. With the introduction of the new 'box' dimensions of 36 feet long by 8 feet 2.5 inches wide, forty-four passengers could now be carried. They were withdrawn in 1974, some three years after the demise of the original C5 types. Thus, Midland Red's most legendary period ended in a blaze of glory, when these last 'homemade' BMMO coaches were used.

Unfortunately, the nearby prosperous car manufacturing companies, in the Birmingham and Coventry areas, kept attracting fitters and craftsmen away from Carlyle Road Works, where wages could be double that paid by Midland Red. This made continued production of in-house manufactured or locally outsourced chassis, engines and bodies increasingly uneconomic. Gradually the manufacturing base in Edgbaston was wound down, with the last coaches (the CM6s) being built in 1966, the last double-decker BMMO D9s also in 1966 and the final S23 single-deck buses in 1970.

Thus, starting in 1965 right through to the end of the Midland Red company as an entire entity in 1981, all the 281 coach chassis bought new were, with one exception, 36-foot-long Leyland Leopard PSU3s, with the majority of the bodies built by Plaxton. The remaining coaches had Willowbrook bodywork. These were all dispersed to Midland Express/Coaches, Midland Red North, East, West and South and many lasted well into the mid-1990s.

After the taking over of the company's Birmingham and Black Country services by West Midland PTE, on 5 December 1973, it left the Midland Red's operational area rather like a Polo Mint – with nothing in the middle. Midland Red then began to acquire operators in the Telford area of Shropshire and in the Cannock region. Their vehicles were not necessarily the most suitable for stage carriage work, but a number were coaches that had reasonable lifespans after their sale to Midland Red.

# The Charabanc Years
## 1919–1930

Midland Red's policy after the First World War was to fit charabanc bodies to the same type of petrol-electric Tilling-Stevens chassis that was employed for ordinary bus work. Gradually this chassis design was developed into the 'homemade' SOS types, specifically built by the company for excursion and longer distance coach work. Midland Red started express coach services in 1921 with routes to Weston-super-Mare and Llandudno. Coach services were gradually expanded around the country and, gradually, the open canvassed-roofed charabancs were replaced with enclosed half-cab coaches. Passengers had to be a hardy breed as journeys with only a rudimentary folding canvas hood for protection in all weathers, and on hard rubber tyres with minimal suspension, on journeys which could take nearly all day to get to, for instance the North Wales seaside resorts, were something of a trial of endurance.

## A102 (OE 1131)

A102 (OE 1131) is a 1919 Tilling-Stevens TS3, uniquely given a charabanc thirty-two-seat body by Collett & MacDonald. It had doors on both sides of the attractively stepped waistline of the body. It is parked in front of a Georgian building in about 1920. In 1926 (OE 1131) was re-registered OE 7315, as the vehicle carrying that registration had been broken up in error, and it was withdrawn in 1927. The Tilling-Stevens TS3 chassis had a 14-foot 6.25-inch wheelbase and were powered by a pair-cast four-cylinder 4.355-litre petrol engine, rated at 40 hp, driving a generator. This provided traction current to an electric motor which drove the bus. Without a clutch and crash gearbox to struggle with, trainee drivers could learn to drive them without too much difficulty. As a result, many newly demobbed soldiers found employment as bus drivers and, by the time the petrol-electric transmission was being replaced by the newer versions of clutch and gearboxes, the drivers were able to adapt to the new method's requirements. OE 1131 was one of a number of charabancs to have the word Midland compacted into the central part of the body, rather than having each letter on each door. (D. R. Harvey Collection)

## 213 (OE 7301)

Church-organised outings seemed to be the order of the day in the early 1920s. Two vicars are going on the ladies' day out, looking to keep a 'fatherly eye' on their flock, who could not expect to have a really good time ... within the acceptable social mores of the day. Former War Department lorry 213 (OE 7301) waits to leave for its day trip into the countryside, where no doubt the stop would be a tearoom, rather than a hostelry. This Tilling-Stevens TS3 was acquired from the War Department in 1920 as a lorry and was quickly fitted with a rather plain, boat-like charabanc body with thirty-two seats that was built by a company called Taylor. This body only had doors on its nearside for each row of seats. The doors on the offside were omitted as a safety measure. (D. R. Harvey Collection)

## 214 (OE 7302)

214 (OE 7302), was a Tilling-Stevens TS3 purchased as a lorry from the War Department and was one of five to receive a thirty-two-seat charabanc body. The body was the only one built for BMMO by Kilner & Brookes, a small local coachbuilder, and was allocated body number C4. In this state it survived until 1926. The word charabanc was adopted into English from the French *char-à-bancs* or *char à bancs* (the hyphens appear to be optional). The literal meaning is 'wagon with benches', and in 1845 it is recorded as meaning 'light two- or four-wheeled vehicle with benches'. The first part (char) is a very old word for a wheeled vehicle of high status, to which the English words car and chariot are related. The form *char-à-bancs* is singular; the plural form is *chars-à-bancs*. (D. R. Harvey Collection)

## 216 (OE 7304)

Parked outside the 1887-built St Mary's Church, in Bearwood, in about 1921, is OE 7304. This normal-control Tilling-Stevens TS3 was new in 1916 and was bought from the War Department in 1920. It was given the number 216 and fitted with a Kilner & Brookes Ch32 body in 1920 and was broken up in 1926. The church's mothers meeting group are off on an excursion. Well hidden amongst the women, who seem to be predominantly grannies, are a few well wrapped-up infants. These private hire day excursions were the very 'bread and butter' trips, which gradually developed into three- and four-day tours. However, this would be a few years later as the comfort of these early vehicles left something to be desired with hard rubber tyres, exposure to the elements and absolutely no heating. (D. R. Harvey Collection)

## 219 (OE 7307)

In the first two years of the 1920s, BMMO tried out some lightweight vehicles in order to attempt to economise. In 1921, a pair of Model T Fords were purchased from Runcimen – a Coventry-based dealer – and fitted with open eleven-seat charabanc bodies, with folding canvass roofs, by a coachbuilder named Thomas Pass. They only lasted until 1924. Despite being underpowered, they were fast and reliable and pointed the way forward for Midland Red's home-produced chassis, which fit the new requirements. (BMMO)

## 234 (OE 7312)

In 1922, three Tilling-Stevens TS3 chassis were bodied by Thomas Startin of, variously, Great Charles Street and Aston Road North. They were a long-established coachbuilder who started building horse-drawn carts in the mid-nineteenth century and progressed into bodying cars. After the end of the First World War, they built a small number of charabancs. Those supplied to BMMO had a seven-row charabanc body with a seating capacity of thirty-two. On the nearside, each row of seats was equipped with its own door, while only one door above the rear wheel was fitted to the offside. 234 (OE 7312), with body number C16, entered service as a normal-control bus in 1922 and was rebodied as a charabanc when only a few months old. The newly rebodied vehicle is well-loaded with a full complement of hardy passengers, who would have to endure the joys of coach travel on a vehicle equipped with rubber tyre wheels. It only ran in this form from 1922 until 1925 before becoming a thirty-two-seat bus. (D. R. Harvey Collection)

## 234 (OE 7312)

The same charabanc again makes an interesting contrast as Tilling-Stevens TS3 234 (OE 7312) is now equipped with pneumatic tyres. The Thomas Startin body for thirty-two passengers now sits higher on the chassis and would make for a far more comfortable ride for them. This all-girls outing has stopped outside a hotel that takes in coach parties for lunches and afternoon teas, which might be why, suitably refreshed, the ladies are actually smiling at the photographer, although the driver, suitably posing in his white driver's coat, does look a little stern. Above the vehicle, on the wall next to the hotel, is a splendid collection of enamelled signs for washing products, such as Hudson's Soap – their laundry soap named Rinso. Both brands were sold to Lever Brothers of Port Sunlight, UK, and, until the 1950s, Rinso was a market leader in mass-marketed soap powders. (D. R. Harvey Collection)

## 241 (HA 2318)

In 1909, the Garford Motor Truck Company was established in Elyria, Ohio, a small town 30 miles outside Cleveland. After building small lorries for the US Army, they began to construct lightweight chassis. A batch of six lightweight Garford 20 hp chassis were imported into the UK and delivered to BMMO, Smethwick, in 1922. They were new with Ch18 Davidson charabanc bodywork and pneumatic tyres and were used at Bearwood (three), Leamington (two) and Worcester (one) garages. There were also fourteen Garfords bodied as buses with B20F or B24F Carlyle bodywork. The charabancs were all withdrawn in 1925 and passed to Winchester & District Motor Services in March 1926. 241 (HA 2318) was the first of the 20 hp Garfords of 1922 and is seen with its canvass roof in the up position, though it would not have given the passengers much protection. (BMMO)

## 262 (E 1843)

About to work on the long-distance service to Llandudno from Seymour Street, off Belgrave Road, Balsall Heath, in Birmingham, is Tilling-Stevens TS3 262 (E 1843). New in 1916, the vehicle was acquired from the Nuneaton-based North Warwickshire Motor Omnibus & Transport Company in February 1918 and fitted with a Tillotson Ch32 body, dating from 1915, which was given the first BMMO coach body number, C1. It lasted in this form until 1925. The radiator had the legend TILLING-STEVENS PETROL ELECTRIC on the header and bottom plates, showing that it was a genuine product of the Maidstone factory. The prospect of going to Llandudno on a hard rubber-tyre, open charabanc with only brakes on the back axle was a daunting prospect for any prospective holiday-goer. Even with the canvas folding roof being extended over the passengers and attaching it to the top of the windscreen, there was hardly any protection for those on board in inclement weather. (D. R. Harvey Collection)

## 359 (HA 2349)

A group of some twenty-four smiling cloche-hatted women pose behind the white-coated Midland Red driver, who sits somewhat casually behind the steering wheel. They are out in the country on a day trip in A359 (HA 2349), a normal-control SOS S-type rebuilt from a Tilling-Stevens TS3 chassis. The bus has a Davidson Ch32 body built at Trafford Park in 1923, who supplied some twenty-seven charabancs to Midland Red between 1923 and 1926. The vehicle is fitted with pneumatic tyres which would have made for a much more comfortable journey. One would have had to have been fairly fit in order to climb up the two sets of plank-like steps along the side of the vehicle. A359 was withdrawn in 1928. (Via P. Tulloch)

## 366 (HA 2353)

This SOS S-type was one of a pair of rebuilt Tilling-Stevens TS3 chassis that were fitted with Davidson thirty-two-seat charabanc bodies and dated from 1923. 366 (HA 2353), had a folding canvas roof which is folded concertina-style at the back of the body. There were six rows of rather plush seats with each row having its own nearside set of doors. Alongside the driver there was a pair of seats in the plum seating position, which also gave them protection behind the windscreen. By now fitted with pneumatic tyres, the charabanc was withdrawn in 1928. (BMMO)

## 367 (HA 2351)

On its way to Blackpool, with a crew of two drivers, SOS S-type 367 (HA 2351), takes a break on its journey. The charabanc, built in 1923, is about halfway through its five-year life span and is equipped with pneumatic tyres. The vehicle was fitted with the SOS 4.344-litre engine, developed with Harry Ricardo-designed cylinder heads, and was a quiet, smooth running side valve petrol unit with a high compression ratio, which was coupled to a four-speed conventional gearbox giving the chassis a good turn of speed. All SOS S types had pneumatic tyres with 36-inch x 8-inch on the front axle and 40-inch x 8-inch on the rear. The vehicle was fitted with a Davidson Ch32 body weighing 3 tonnes 13 cwt. HA 2351 had the body number C30. Alas the charabanc-type body had not kept up with this chassis development in terms of comfort and weather protection. The protection was limited to a canvas roof supported by vertical struts that fitted into the lower body frame at seven mounting points. The last true charabancs built on SOS S-type chassis were built by Midland Red in 1927 for the Llandudno Coaching & Carriage Company. (D. R. Harvey Collection)

## 399 (HA 2354)

399 (HA 2354) was a BMMO S-type built in 1924 using Tilling-Stevens TS3 frames but with the substitution of a clutch and gearbox for the previous petrol-electric transmission. The body style was slightly lower and somewhat better looking than the first charabancs, despite the windscreen still being below the face of the driver thus affording him minimum protection when driving. Although at an unknown location standing across the gated entrance to perhaps a country mansion, these Midland excursions were very well patronised with vehicles being loaded to the gunwales in order to make the trip profitable. This party of mainly middle-aged couples look sternly towards the photographer prior to returning home. The charabanc, HA 2354, survived in service until 1928. (D. R. Harvey Collection)

## 499 (HA 2438)

Entering service in May 1925 as BMMO 499 (HA 2438) had a Davidson Ch32 body mounted on an SOS S-type normal-control chassis and with pneumatic tyres from new. It was given the body number C41 but was sold to Northern General in 1927 where it became 336 in their fleet. As part of the modernisation of the body – although it retained its folding canvas roof – it was given glass side windows which gave everyone on board a much warmer ride. NGT bought its first SOS chassis in 1924 and bought its last new ones in 1934. After a brief sojourn with the NGT-associated Wakefield's Motors of Tynemouth, HA 2438 returned to the parent company as 591 in 1933 and was scrapped in May 1935. (NGT)

## 636 (HA 3525)

The nearside of the forward control SOS FS charabanc 636 (HA 3525) shows all seven doors to the upholstered bench seats. There is now a proper windscreen for the driver as well as front bulkhead screens for the passengers. At the rear of the body is the canvas roof, which, when pulled forward, would protect the driver and the passengers alike. Although the tyres at the rear are larger than those at the front, they are only single ones, making the vehicle look a little spindly on its pins! The charabanc is parked in front of an impressive set of entrance gates at an unknown location. (OS)

## 641 (HA 3526)

British Camp is an Iron Age hill fort located at the top of Herefordshire Beacon in the Malvern Hills. The summit of British Camp (1,109 feet) has been a tourist spot since the late eighteenth century. The hill fort is protected as a scheduled ancient monument and is owned and maintained by Malvern Hills Conservators. The fort is thought to have been first constructed in the second century BC and lasted until the middle of the first century AD. A Norman castle was later built on the site but was finally destroyed by King Henry II in 1155. 641 (HA 3526), a Davidson Ch34-bodied SOS FS, is on an educational outing from Birmingham to British Camp in the Malvern Hills in the late 1920s. (T. J. Edgington)

## 658 (HA 3528)

Yet another works outing! Midland Red began to get a good foothold into the annual factory day out market by the mid-1920s. 658 (HA 3528), a Davidson-bodied thirty-four-seat charabanc mounted on a 1926 SOS FS forward control chassis, is well loaded with both men and women, all of whom are wearing hats! The large folding roof at the rear must have been awfully heavy and difficult to put up quickly and of course there was little or no side protection for the passengers in bad weather. (D. R. Harvey Collection)

## 667 (HA 3666)

667 (HA 3666) was the prototype SOS QC with a Carlyle Ch30 body built at the BMMO Works at Carlyle Road, Edgbaston, in 1927. It remained in service for nine years. Only nineteen of these charabancs were built, of which five were constructed for Trent Motor Traction. The body had a single hinged door near to the front of the body and were the last coaches to have just rear wheel brakes. The vehicles had the original SOS four-cylinder 4.344-litre petrol engine, but the lightweight 4 tonnes 3 cwt body enabled the coach to have a good turn of speed. (BMMO)

## 721 (HA 3671)

Parked on the Marine Parade on Weston-super-Mare sea front on a warm day in July 1928, is 721 (HA 3671), a 1927 SOS QC. The QC model (Queen Charabanc) was the company's first touring coach and reverted to a normal-control configuration. The QC had thirty seats with bodywork by Carlyle and weighed 4 tonnes 3 cwt. They had the advantage of a fixed rear dome and a sliding canvas roof, permanent side windows, a central gangway and quite luxurious seating, which can be seen through the open front door. (D. R. Harvey Collection)

## 798 (HA 4823)

The Queen Low Charabanc was an improved version of the SOS QC and initially entered service in 1928. They were bodied with Ch29 bodies, but this time built by Short Brothers of Rochester in Kent. The bodywork was virtually identical to the QC, but the chassis had four-wheel brakes, which were identifiable by the plate front wheels that had replaced the earlier spoked wheels. Not every trip to Weston-super-Mare was undertaken on a sunny day. Here the woman standing by the front door is wearing a stylish 1920s hat and a fur collared coat. The vehicle's canvas roof has been put up and battened down onto the cant rail above the permanent glass side windows using the fixing studs. Perhaps this photograph really captures the trials and tribulations of a day trip to the seaside by charabancs. The vehicle, along with all the other 1928 Midland Red four-cylinder QLC, was sold in 1935 to Northern General. (G. Davies)

## 807 (HA 4830)

807 (HA 4830) was one of the 1928-built SOS QLC touring coaches. It is standing in front of an unidentifiable public house when on a day trip. The coach has a party of mainly flat-capped men although there are at least eight cloche-hatted women. The side-fixed windows on the Short CH 29 body gave a certain amount of protection and the canvas roof is furled away into the top of the fixed rear dome. These vehicles had equal-sized tyres, which enabled the body height to be reduced by three inches to 8 feet 2 inches. (D. R. Harvey Collection)

## 1002 (HA 5025)

Standing in front of the King's Head, Bearwood, only about 400 yards from the Midland Red headquarters, is 1002 (HA 5025), with its capped and white-coated driver sitting behind the well raked steering wheel. This was one of the twenty six-cylinder SOS QLC touring coaches bodied with a Short Ch29 body to enter service in 1929. They had the new SOS 5.047-litre SS-type engine, located behind the modern, smooth-sided radiator with the word MIDLAND on the header tank. Just visible through the crack in the original negative is a Birmingham Corporation AEC Regent 661 with a piano-front body dating from 1930, daring the tear of the photograph really well. 1002 was withdrawn in 1938 but spent three years on loan to Potteries Motor Traction. (D. R. Harvey Collection)

## 1013 (HA 5035)

Fillongley is a village in North Warwickshire between Coleshill and Bedworth. It was in this village in about 1932 that the Parish Church of St Mary and All Saints had arranged for a coach trip in a Midland Red 'chara'. The ladies of the church were off to have a good time and 1013 (HA 5035), a six-cylinder SOS QLC touring coach bodied by Short Brothers with a Ch29 body dating from 1929, waits for the last posed photograph to be taken before starting its journey. One must assume that the lady with briefcase is the trip organiser and who is carrying booking forms, the list of passengers and the itinerary. (D. R. Harvey Collection)

## 1178 (HA 5144)

The last BMMO charabancs were built in 1930 and were Short-bodied SOS QLC six-cylinder twenty-nine-seater normal-control vehicles, which still retained the canvas folding roof. By the end of the 1920s, this feature was rapidly falling out of fashion and within a year a new broom of modernity would sweep through the Midland Red design office. Despite having the new smooth outlined radiator, front wheel brakes, a six-cylinder 5.047-litre engine and twin rear tyres, they were really outdated when compared to contemporary AEC Regals and Leyland Tiger models. The vehicle is parked near to Leicester's Southgate Street garage. (W. J. Haynes)

# Early Half-Cab Coaches
# 1930–1935

Midland Red's foray into the forward control, half-cab era was something of a disaster. A completely new chassis developed from the late 1920s. SOS MM and IM bus chassis were introduced as the XL-type, but with a lightweight chassis and a modern-looking luxury body, they quickly gained a reputation for being under-powered, top heavy, too heavy and unstable. The coach bodies were placed on the new, heavier RR-type chassis, while within a year the XL chassis received new lighter bodies intended for other chassis. This latter combination became the SOS MM six-cylinder bus. It was one of the rare occasions when the Midland Red vehicle building policy of a lightweight chassis and a modern, powerful and good-sized petrol engine, coupled to a lightweight body, really failed the company. This failure probably set their coaching activities back by a couple of years while the reputation of their coaches recovered. Despite these problems, the geographical area of the coaching activities was substantially increased and in 1934 Midland Red became a founder member of the Associated Motorways consortium. During the mid-1930s, Midland Red surprisingly constructed two batches of normal-control touring coaches, which was rather against the current trend in new coaches of this layout as other operators were phasing them out.

## 1049 (HA 4960)
SOS RR 1049 (HA 4960) is parked at Carlyle Road Works with Edgbaston Reservoir behind the coach when new in 1930. The design was quite modern though hardly harmonious with the front end of the vehicle looking very antiquated when compared to the curved tumblehome of the saloon. A Brush C30F body was fitted to this XL chassis and was designed for long-distance coaching work but was transferred to a new 1930 SOS RR chassis because the body was too heavy, mainly due to its luxury fixtures and fittings. The open front door reveals the luxurious plush red leather seats and the curtains attached to the interior of the body pillars. The RRs had the SOS six-cylinder 6.373-litre petrol engine, which gave the coach a good performance and was ideal for coaching activities. The original XL chassis was rebuilt as an SOS MM six-cylinder vehicle and re-registered HA 5055. (BMMO)

## 1090 (HA 4999)

The SOS XL was the first vehicle designed by BMMO as a long-distance coach. It had the QLC-style radiator and a six-cylinder SOS 5.047-litre SS-type. Built in 1929, XL chassis proved to be somewhat lightweight so their Carlyle C30F bodywork was placed on the new RR-type chassis the following year and renumbered 1225. Waiting to board HA 4999 is a vicar, his wife and their dog at Cheltenham coach station when virtually new in its rebuilt state. The bodies were equipped with a shallow roof luggage rack. These buses were the first to have a new design of a flat-topped header tank with the letters MIDLAND inscribed on it. The RRs had a new livery of red below the waistrail, and maroon above, including the waistrail, roof and window surrounds. The RR chassis, with their SOS 6.373-litre petrol engines, had a performance comparable to vehicles manufactured by AEC, Dennis or Leyland. With half-cabs, all-round brakes, an enclosed saloon with plush seating they also were equipped with a roof-mounted luggage rack. One oddity, however, which lasted throughout the pre-war period, was the fuel tank was not positioned between the wheelbase, but underneath the driver's seat in the cab. (A. Ingram)

## 1189 (HA 4963)

With the crew posing in front of 1189 (HA 4963), this SOS RR of 1930 has a 1929 Brush C30F body that was lavishly appointed, but which proved to be too heavy for their original XL chassis. As re-chassied, the RR had a six-cylinder 6.373-litre petrol engine and weighed 5 tonnes 12 cwt, making them the heaviest SOS vehicle to be built. It is parked in Coventry and retains the original front route boards, which reveal that the coach is working on the service to Leicester. A feature of the bodywork on these coaches was the curved bulkhead window above the acetylene nearside of the half-cab. (R. Wilson)

## 1198 (HA 4960)

Parked at a break point on the service between Birmingham and London is 1198 (HA 4960). This SOS RR chassis was new in 1930 and had a Brush C30F body removed from the unsuccessful 1929 SOS XL chassis formerly fitted to 1049. The RR chassis had a 16-foot 7.5-inch wheelbase, the new RR2LB six-cylinder 6.373-litre petrol engine and smaller 34-inch x 7-inch tyres all round. The bodywork had, for the first time, a fitted roof as well as retaining the roller blind front destination box – a feature that was not repeated on BMMO single-deckers until after the end of the Second World War. 1198 was withdrawn in 1944. (D. R. Harvey Collection)

## 1208 (HA 4992)

1208 (HA 4992) was extensively modernised in the mid-1930s, although, despite its better appearance, apparently it was the only one to be rebuilt. A new deeper roof was fitted, when in conjunction with the unaltered saloon windows, and the new longer body side panels really upgraded the appearance of the Brush bodywork on this SOS RR. The coach is parked in Bromsgrove and is still in its original coach livery though it was possibly being used for bus work. (R. T. Coxon)

## 1231 (HA 4971)

Posing in front of 1231 (HA 4971) in Oxford's Gloucester Green bus station is a smartly dressed mother and her two sons, who are both in their school uniforms. The bus is a SOS RR of 1930 that had been fitted with a 1929 Brush C30F body from the successful XL chassis. It was eventually taken out of service in 1943 after being on loan to Potteries Motor Traction since 1940. The bus has the rounded style of radiator, which rather emphasised the narrow width of the windscreen – a characteristic feature of all the 1930s SOS chassis. (D. R. Harvey Collection)

## 1233 (HA 4991)

SOS RR 1233 (HA 4991) is fresh out of Carlyle Road Works and stands in the yard at the rear of the works, with Edgbaston Reservoir behind the coach. The body came from an SOS XL and was designed for long-distance coaching, as exemplified by the Birmingham to Llandudno slip board that is attached to the roof-mounted luggage rack. The open front door reveals the luxurious plush red leather seats and the curtains attached to the interior of the body pillars. The RRs had the SOS six-cylinder 6.373-litre petrol engine, which gave the coach a good performance that was ideal for coaching activities. Coach 1233 was eventually taken out of service in 1944. (BMMO)

## 1238 (RF 3348)

1238 (RF 3348) was the only coach taken over with the Black Country services of the Great Western Railway on 23 May 1930. Originally numbered 1598 in the GWR fleet, it was originally new to F. E. Weston (Blue Bus) of Cradley Heath. The canvas-roofed half-cab was a Maudslay ML3A and had a Birmingham-built Buckingham C32F body. Although it was only three years old, it definitely looked like last year's coach. It only stayed with Midland Red for a few months before being sold to Western National as their 3051. (D. R. Harvey Collection)

## 1243 (HA 6174)

In 1930, twelve SOS SRR coaches were constructed, of which only two went to BMMO, the balance going to Northern General. They had Short C30F bodies which were very similar to SOD-S RRs, but without a luggage roof rack. They had front destination roller blinds which also had provision for wooden slip boards. Both the Midland Red pair had five-speed overdrive gearboxes. 1243 (HA 6174) is working on the long X96 service from Northampton and Shrewsbury by way of Rugby, Coventry, Meriden, Birmingham, Dudley, Wolverhampton, Wellington and Shrewsbury and a one-way journey took five and a half hours to complete. Although this was a limited stop express service, coaches were always used. HA 6174 is parked in Pool Meadow bus station, in August 1939, within weeks of the outbreak of the Second World War, and, as such, routes were compulsorily suspended from 1 September 1942. With fuel rationing beginning on 23 September 1939, many excursions and coach services were severely restricted. (R. T. Coxon)

## 1499 (HA 9051)

The prototype SOS LRR was HA 9051, later given the fleet A number 1499. It had a Short C30F body and was built in 1933 and had a thin tapering driver's cab. This new design of coach was like nothing else built by Midland Red or any other coachbuilder at the time. To state that the body design was eccentric would be an understatement! This was the only LRR to have a five-speed gearbox. The driver's cab was raised above the passenger saloon in the same way as the SOS REDD double-deckers and had a double-decker back axle and transmission. With the demise of wartime coach work, it was converted to a B34F layout in 1941. As a bus it is parked in the early post-war years. It was withdrawn in 1950. (D. R. Harvey Collection)

## 1643 (AHA 588)

The production batch of SOS LRR coaches numbered thirty-one vehicles, of which just one went to Potteries Motor Traction. The 1934 batch were numbered 1586–1590, while another twenty-five were delivered in 1935. These were the first new coaches built by BMMO since the SRR vehicles and were a radical departure from earlier Midland Red coaches. The LRRs were well made luxurious coaches and weighed 5 tonnes 16 cwt unladen. Sometimes the avant garde or adventurous design features quickly lose their novelty value. But in some ways the design was just strangely proportioned and perhaps, had it not been for their conversion into service buses, they might have had an even shorter life. They were all converted into B34F buses and in this form lasted until 1951. 1643 (AHA 588) is parked alongside the River Medway near to Short's factory in Rochester, Kent, when new and in its pomp has been painted in the distinct elaborately lined-out livery. (A. Ingram)

## 1651(AHA 596)

Immediately after it had been converted to a single-decker, SOS LRR 1651 (AHA 596) stands on the cobbles in Huntingdon Street bus station in 1942. The elaborate pre-war livery had gone to be replaced by an all-over red scheme. The bus has a full set of wartime white-edging and headlight masks and had extra side-facing seats over the rear wheel arches, enabling the seating capacity to increase by four to B34F after its conversion in 1941. Despite being stripped of all its luxury fittings, the unusually styled SOS LRRs could barely concede their coaching origins. 1651 continued in service until 1951. The class were replaced by BMMO S12 underfloor engined buses. (G. H. F. Atkins)

## 1655 (AHA 600)

Standing between a couple of Maidstone & District Leyland Tigers is 1655 (AHA 600). The SOS LRR design was considerably lower than these Leylands, which were among the most advanced coaches in operation in the United Kingdom. Their Short C30C bodies, with the radiused corners on the bottom of the saloon windows, looked splendid in their red livery and yellow window surrounds with black wings and gold lining out! The smart radiator, with MIDLAND embossed on the header tank and SOS lettering on the centre line of the radiator, gives an impression of quality as the coach waits to continue its journey in 1935. It is on hire to London Coastal Coaches Limited, which was formed in the summer of 1925. It was this company who organised using their own and other operator's coaches to the south coast, Kent, Essex and East Anglia. (D. R. Harvey Collection)

## 1663 (AHA 608)

In 1934 Midland Red became a founder member of the Associated Motorways consortium. They did not own or operate any coaches. Each member company committed itself to providing an agreed mileage of coach journeys for Associated Motorways and took an agreed share of the profits. The consortium initially included Black & White Motorways, Crosville, Eastern Counties, Bristol Greyhound, Lincolnshire Road Car, Midland Red, Red & White, Royal Blue, Southdown and United Counties. Surrounded by Bristol, Gloster and Gilford chassied coaches, BMMO's 1663 (AHA 608), one of the SOS LRRs of 1935, is parked in Cheltenham's then revolutionary coach station in St Margaret's Road, which opened in 1931 and was the hub of the Associated Motorways group. It is about 1936 and the revolutionary undercover coach station sees the usual wandering passengers looking for their coach to take them on to their destination. The white painted window frames emphasise the higher level of the driver's strangely shaped cab, seemingly perching above the rest of the Short-built bodywork. (Cheltenham Bus Preservation Group)

## 1668 (AHA 612) and 1674 (AHA 618)

After a day trip to Rhyl on the North Wales Coast, three normal-control Short C29F bodied SOS OLRs are on their way back to Birmingham. Only two of them, 1668 (AHA 612) and 1674 (AHA 618), are identifiable when parked at the Raven Inn on the A41 near Prees Heath. This was a favourite refreshment stop for most coach operators going to the North Wales seaside resorts. The OLRs were normal-control coaches, whose layout had all but been abandoned in the very early 1930s and at that time were only built to special order in penny numbers. They were designed as touring coaches and with their striking lined-out red and yellow livery also sported a roll-back canvas roof enabling them to operate as open-toppers. They were fitted with the SOS RR2LB 6.373-litre petrol engine and FEDD front and rear axles. (G. Davies)

## 1689 (AHA 634)

Seen on a day excursion, 1689 (AHA 634) is parked at an unknown location when still fairly new. The weather must have been not too kind as the coach has its canvas roof buttoned down, though it does not look very taut as the roof sticks are clearly visible. These SOS OLRs, with Short C29C bodywork, were the last normal-control chassis to be built by Midland Red and were roughly contemporary to the normal-control Leyland Tigress coaches built for Southdown and Devon General. They were among the last of this chassis layout to enter service in the UK in the late 1930s. (R. T. Coxon)

## 1691 (AHA 636)

The twenty-five SOS OLRs of 1935 must have been some of the most radically altered vehicles to be rebuilt during the Second World War. 1691 (AHA 636) is parked in Digbeth garage yard in about 1947 and is completely unrecognisable from its original guise. It is now a thirty-four-seat forward control bus and has been fitted with a fully integrated roof. There is hardly a vestige of its normal-control touring coach days left, save for the elaborately styled front and rear mudguards, the large numbers of saloon windows and the curvature of the roof line towards the rear of the body. They retained the rather attractive radiator that were unique to the OLRs. (D. R. Harvey Collection)

## JF 4874

The Leicester & District Company, known as Leicester Green, bought mainly Albion chassis and operated from Leicester via the A6 to Quorn and Loughborough. The last of the twenty-three coaches to be bought by the company was JF 4874, in July 1933, and when the company was taken over this Duple C35F-bodied Albion PV70 was one of just six vehicles from the Leicester Green fleet to be briefly operated. It is in Bearwood garage in 1937, having been taken over by Midland Red in 1936, and has been given the Midland Red fleet name but still retains the old company's green livery. Despite this attention to detail, JF 4874 was given the A number 1967 and was sold during the following year. (D. R. Harvey Collection)

# Advanced Art Deco Coaches
# of the Late 1930s

During the late 1930s Midland Red began to produce quite amazingly advanced rear-engined single-deckers. One of the four produced was a coach that was registered CHA 2. The streamlined avant garde bodywork was built at Carlyle Road Works and was designed in a distinctly Art Deco style. Although the chassis was chronically unreliable, the rounded full-fronted bodywork had an influence on the bodies built on the mechanically less adventurous front-engined SOS SLRs of 1937, and the SOS ONCs introduced in the last year before the Second World War.

## 1942 (CHA 1)
Of the four experimental SOS RECs built between May 1935 and 1937, only the second one, CHA 1, was bodied as a coach, its streamlined body being built by Carlyle with a C32C layout. It had a SOS 6.373-litre rear-mounted petrol engine that was coupled to a French-built Cotal epicyclic semi-automatic gearbox, unusually operated electromagnetically through a Daimler fluid flywheel. By May 1940, CHA 1 was off the road. The chronic unreliability of the coach resulted in it rarely venturing beyond the range of a day excursion from Bearwood garage. With the outbreak of war and the unavailability of obtaining parts from France, it was withdrawn in May 1940 after being delicensed for some two years. The streamlined body was sold to Hardwick of Bilston, who fitted it to Leyland Tiger registration number KF 4726. A new chassis with an underfloor engine was constructed using the same type of horizontal 8.028-litre engine as fitted to BHA 1, the first rear-engined conversion. The gearbox was a spare four-speed ZF Aphon unit of the type purchased in 1938 and used in SOS FEDD and SON chassis. CHA 1 used the same and received a new Carlyle-built seven-bay B40F body and was given the chassis type designation S2 and fleet number 1942. It was withdrawn in 1957. (Motor Transport)

## 1968–2017 class

There were at least ten visible SOS SLR chassis having their composite bodywork constructed at the English Electric erecting shop, in Preston, during 1937. Midland Red surprisingly ordered 215 single-deck bus bodies, on SOS SON chassis, from English Electric, in three batches between 1936 and 1938; one double-deck body on an SOS FEDD; and fifty bodies for the SOS SLRs. The Lancashire body builder had got these contracts because one of Midland Red's previous bodybuilders, Shorts of Rochester, in Kent, had ceased bus building to concentrate on the construction of flying boats. English Electric had built bus bodies since about 1930 but latterly their bodywork had to be recalled to Preston for rectification work. This was due to poor design and construction methods. Although the SLR coach bodies were rebuilt in time for the first post-war tourist season, the company seemed to regard them quite well, although, perhaps significantly, the body order for the SOS ONCs went to Duple. (D. R. Harvey Collection)

## 1968 (CHA 950)

The first of the SOS SLR coaches was 1968 (CHA 950). Built in 1937, it was withdrawn in 1955. It was sold to AMCC Ltd of Stratford, in east London, and was subsequently exported to an unknown operator in Limassol on the Mediterranean island of Cyprus. The coach, now registered TQ 865, is parked in the town of Varosha near to the southern quarter of Famagusta on 6 November 1959. This was when Varosha was one of the most popular seaside tourist resorts on the island. Following the Turkish invasion of Cyprus, on 20 July 1974, its inhabitants fled to Larnaca, across the UN Green Line, and the town has remained uninhabited and totally abandoned and fenced off ever since. (G. Pattison)

## 1975 (CHA 957)

In 1937, fifty new full-fronted C30C coaches were introduced with concealed radiators, a sliding centre door and a stepped waistrail enabling the passengers at the rear of the coach to get a better view to the front. These were the SOS SLRs which had English Electric bodywork. EE were at the time supplying bodies to Midland Red on the SOS SON buses in the DHA registration series. Despite appearances, the SLR was derived from the normal-control OLR-type of 1935. It had a 17-foot x 6-foot wheelbase, double-decker-type axles and an underslung differential. Unusually for a 1930s SOS chassis, the fuel tank was mounted conventionally on the offside of the chassis frame. Rebuilt in the 1947–8 period with a simplified livery, they also received a simplified waterfall radiator grill. The SLR designation stood for Saloon Low Rolls-Royce. 1975 (CHA 957) is parked in about 1948 in company with an un-rebuilt SOS FEDD, an un-rebuilt Duple-bodied wartime Daimler CWA6 and a 1949 AD2-type Metro-Cammell-bodied AEC Regent II. (D. R. Harvey Collection)

## 1983 (CHA 965)

After their withdrawal from coach work, two of the SOS SLRs were converted to dual control driver trainers in 1955. 1983 (CHA 965) lasted in this role until 1961, although its twin, 1980 (CHA 962), remained as a trainee vehicle until 1963. 1983 is parked near to the Midland Railway entrance to New Street station in Station Street, Birmingham. Both were painted in an all-over red livery, with the driving instructor sitting on the nearside of the full-front cab with his own steering wheel, clutch and hand and foot brake. The two decommissioned coaches were allocated to the Midland Red Driving School based at Bearwood garage and they were both to be seen musically pottering around Birmingham as the driver under instruction attempted to master their four-speed gearboxes. (D. R. Harvey Collection)

## 1991 (CHA 973)

In Gran Canaria, with the local operator APJG, is an English Electric C30F-bodied SOS SLR formerly number 1991 (CHA 973). It is, by now, numbered 20 GC9680 in their fleet. Withdrawn by BMMO in 1955, CHA 973 was sold to APJC along with a number of other SLRs. This SLR had been re-engined in 1947 with a Leyland E181 7.4-litre diesel engine and due to this those exported to the Canary Islands were basically regarded as Leyland Tigers. Once the SOS SLRs had been exported to APJG, the original centre exit was panelled over and replaced by one on what was now the nearside of the coach. (J. C. Cockshott)

## 1994 (CHA 976)

Loading up with passengers in Hereford bus station, 1994 (CHA 976), one of the SOS SLRs with English Electric C30C bodywork, stands with its driver already behind the steering wheel and ready to leave. It is 13 August 1939 and within three weeks everything would change and never be quite the same again as war would have been declared on Germany. The coach is in its original livery, being painted all-over red with brown mudguards and body styling flash. A neat touch was the white pointers on the tapered body pillars, which brought just a bit more style to the appearance of the SLR coaches. The bus sports an original Art Deco radiator grill, which was most attractive but difficult to maintain and keep polished. (OS)

## 1996 (CHA 978)

Parked on the forecourt of Digbeth garage yard is 1996 (CHA 978), an English Electric C30C-bodied SOS SLR dating from 1937. The body style had echoes of the Carlyle body fitted to the solitary SOS REC coach. 1996 stands alongside the slightly lower-build of 2279 (FHA 411) – one of the twenty-five SOS ONCs with a Duple C30C body dating from 1939. The SLR had been re-engined with a Leyland E181 7.4-litre oil engine, in 1947, when it was reupholstered from green, which general manager Donald Sinclair didn't like, into the more usual black and red colours. (D. R. Harvey Collection)

## 1999 (CHA 981)

Turning into Buckingham Palace Road, near to Victoria coach station, London, soon after being overhauled and repainted is 1999 (CHA 981). All fifty of the SOS SLRs entered service in 1937 and had English Electric C30C bodywork. In its simplified black and red livery, and a more harmonious use of the aluminium brightwork, the whole effect belied the age of the coach. As part of their post-war refurbishment, all the SLRs were re-engined with the Leyland E.181 7.4-litre diesel engine – in the case of 1999 this occurred in 1948. As with all the other SLRs, 1999 would be retired in 1955. (S. N. J. White)

## 2012 (CHA 994)

English Electric C30C-bodied SOS SLRs of 1937 were used on express service work during the early part of the Second World War. They retained their pre-war livery but had their front wings painted white to assist other motorists and pedestrians in the blackout. The bottoms of the rear and side panels were also painted white and the head lights were fitted with the compulsory headlight masks. The side lights were also masked with just an open pinprick available to assist other road users. All SLRs had 17-foot 6-inch wheelbases and were powered by the SOS RR2 6.373-litre petrol engine until 1948. 2012 (CHA 994) is parked in Glasshouse Street, in Nottingham, in August 1940. The coach would lose its Art Deco radiator grill. It was re-engined in 1947. (G. H. F. Atkins)

## 2269 (FHA 401)

As a double-decker speeds past, Duple-bodied SOS ONC is barkering in potential customers for an afternoon tour costing 3/6d or the evening Mystery Tour for the same price. The coach is in the post-war plain red with black roof livery and compares well with the late 1940s Leyland Tiger PS2 parked alongside it. Coaches strategically parked with advertising placards in front of them were a fairly cheap method of getting prospective passengers to go on a coach trip with usually a stop-off for a cup of tea halfway through the journey. 2269 was initially withdrawn in 1958 but along with three other ONCs it survived until the end of the 1960 season having been replaced by the new BMMO C5 coaches. (D. R. Harvey Collection)

## 2272 (FHA 404)

A line of four SOS ONC coaches stand in front of a distant row of miscellaneous vehicles in Birmingham in 1949. This number of coaches would suggest a works outing. The leading coach is 2272 (FHA 404), which had a twenty-one-year service life, not being withdrawn until 1960. The Duple-bodied ONCs were fitted from new with the new SOS K-type oil engine which had a capacity of 8.028 litres. This was coupled to a ZF Aphon four-speed gearbox with overdrive and the resulting vehicle gave a rather sophisticated ride. The ONCs had the same single-deck overhead worm drive back axle as the corresponding SON single-deck buses. (R. K. Cope)

## 2273 (FHA 405)

How the mighty have fallen! 2273 (FHA 405) was converted to a dual-control driver training bus in 1960 with a duplicate set of controls, including steering wheel and clutch and brake pedals, in the nearside of the full-front Duple body for use by the driving instructor. Midland Red always took their driver instruction very seriously. After a week's course, the trainee was taken out on Midland Red's own driving test, and after passing would then go on to their allocated garage for further 'type training'. Then they were let loose! It was painted all-over red and had its destination boxes painted over. It is in Leamington Spa garage yard being given a hose-down. (D. R. Harvey Collection)

## 2276 (FHA 408)

Parked outside a Watney, Combe & Reid-owned public house when on its way towards Victoria coach station is 2276 (FHA 408). The driver of this Duple-bodied SOS ONC is adjusting something in the cab of his coach, whose body is only about half full of passengers. As was usually the case with Midland Red, the coach was immaculately turned out for the journey, which was timetabled to take five and a half hours (in the days before the advent of the motorway links) via Stratford-upon-Avon, Banbury, Bicester, Aylesbury and Watford, and all for the return price of 20/- or £1. (D. R. Harvey Collection)

## 2277 (FHA 409)

Journey's end! Having come all the way from Kidderminster, no doubt the day trippers on 2277 (FHA 409) would have hoped for better weather in Blackpool. Parked at Rigby Road coach station behind the SOS ONC is a Weymann dual-purpose-bodied Leyland Tiger PS1/1, owned by Crosville, while on the right is an unidentified ECW full-front-bodied Bristol LWL coach, owned by a BTC Group operator. Still there would always be fish and chips, the pubs and the Pleasure Beach fair ground to entertain the visitors despite the weather, so all would not be lost! (H. Peers)

## 2282 (FHA 414)

Returning from a day out at Ascot Races in 1953 is SOS ONC 2282 (FHA 414). This Duple-bodied coach is carrying decorative Coronation flags as it is around the time of the Queen's Coronation. It also has the number 2 in the windscreen, suggesting the vehicle is one of several coaches being used on that year's new coach. A conductor is just inside the central exit doors. FHA 414 is in the post-war livery with the lower panels painted red with a black roof and window frames. The dour looking faces of the passengers suggest than not too many winners had been backed. (D. R. Harvey Collection)

## 2286 (FHA 418)

SOS ONC 2286 (FHA 418), was retained by Midland Red for special duties as it had a sliding open roof and could be used for special occasions. As far as Leicester City FC was concerned it wasn't a very lucky vehicle, as it was used by them after the cup finals of May 1961 and May 1963, which were both lost! 2286 is being used as a decorated float for a parade with the losing team through the streets of Leicester in front of their fans. This is the 1963 parade, which took place on 26 May 1963 after Leicester lost 3-1 to Manchester United. It would also be one of 2286's last duties as it was withdrawn soon afterwards. Perhaps this was just as well for Leicester City! (D. R. Harvey Collection)

## 2291 (FHA 423)

Leaving the dark confines of Digbeth coach station in Birmingham, en route to Bournemouth in 1959, is 2291 (FHA 423), a Duple-bodied ONC (onward coach) dating from 1939. The only clue to its front-engined chassis layout is the large radiator, otherwise these coaches could be easily mistaken for the post-war C1 coaches. The coach has the red and black post-war livery which does enhance its more modern appearance. 2291 was in its last year of service, being withdrawn in 1960. These last ONCs were still in use when the first BMMO C5 coaches entered service. (J. C. Cockshott)

## 2293 (FHA 425)

Despite their sleek and modern appearance, the SOS ONCs reverted to having their fuel filler caps at the front of the nearside of the coach. Strictly speaking 2293 (FHA 425), the last of the SOS ONCs, was a LON-type (luxury onward) and was allocated to Bearwood garage for use as the director's coach with a reduced seating capacity and tables. It was used throughout the Second World War in this capacity and only entered the normal operating fleet in 1949. It was withdrawn in September 1960 along with most of the rest of the ONCs. (D. R. Harvey Collection)

# Early Post-War Coaches
## 1948–1950

Midland Red's re-entry into the post-war coach market was indeed dramatic. The BMMO C1 carried forward the pre-war SOS ONC body styling but it now had an underfloor horizontal engine. Overnight it made the contemporary half-cab coaches built by AEC, Bristol, Daimler, Crossley, Guy and Daimler look old-fashioned. Yet it would be another three years before these large manufacturers caught up with their own underfloor engine designs. Between 1948 and 1949, sixty-five BMMO C1 coaches were constructed by Duple, with thirty-seat bodies, to the then maximum dimensions of 27 feet 6 inches long and 7 feet 6 inches wide. In 1950, a further twelve touring coaches classified C2 entered service with a reduced seating layout for just twenty-six passengers. These coaches had long lives and most remained in service until the mid-1960s. A number received new bodies in 1962, which gave them nearly another decade in service, while some became dual-control trainers and replaced a comparable number of pre-war SOS SLRs that had been adapted for this purpose in the mid-1950s.

### Duple factory 1949)
Standing inside the doors of the Duple factory in Hendon, approaching completion in 1949, are three vehicles. On the right is a Guy Arab III with the fleet number 13 and a very British destination blind showing ACACIA AVENUE. Note the dual entrance body is fitted with tropical saloon ventilators above the windscreen. This thirty-six-seater was for the Rhodesia OC, Bulawayo, and would be registered B 13669. The vehicle on the left is more difficult to identify but also appears to be a Guy Arab III with a full-front coach body for a northern Europe operator. Between the two is an early BMMO C1 almost ready for delivery. It is missing its front grill and is therefore not identifiable. (A. N. Porter)

## 3300 (KHA 300)

The first of the forty-five-strong class of Duple C30C-bodied BMMO C1s was 3300 (KHA 300). It entered service in April 1949 just in time for the start of the touring season and, with its body built to Midland Red's specification, it must have been a sensation. The Duple bodies were 27 feet 6 inches long and 7 feet 6 inches wide and weighed 6 tonnes 18¾ cwts. The body design of these underfloor-engined coaches was a development from the 1939 SOS ONCs and with the slightly mid-Atlantic style of radiator grill, the overall effect was both tasteful and restrained. During their long lifetime, most of these coaches were placed in winter storage with 3300 being taken out of service during its sixteen-year career no less than fourteen times. 3300 remained in service until September 1965. (D. Williams)

## 3301 (KHA 301)

3301 (KHA 301) was the only Duple-bodied BMMO C1 to be delivered during 1948, entering service in the November of that year and, as shown by the cantrail slip board, was used latterly by the Midland Red Concert Orchestra. 3301 was first taken out of service in May 1963 and was converted to a C24C layout for use by the members of the orchestra and their instruments. In this condition it was repainted in standard coach fleet livery and, in this new role, looked really smart. After it was finally withdrawn in 1971, KHA 301 was fortunate enough to be purchased by the 3301 Preservation Group. (D. R. Harvey Collection)

### 3307 (KHA 307)

The complete family of Midland Red coaches built between 1939 and 1959 are parked in the Eastern Counties garage yard in Great Yarmouth. 3307 (KHA 307) was eventually withdrawn in October 1964 and re-entered service in January 1965 fitted with dual control for driver training. In this guise it was used until February 1971. A trip from Birmingham to Great Yarmouth in the 1950s would have taken just over eight and a half hours. Alongside it is BMMO C5 4793 (793 GHA), which had entered service in August 1959 and faced a twelve-year service life. The third coach is 2272 (FHA 404), a 1939 Duple-bodied SOS ONC with a front engine hidden behind a full front body. As a result, the ONCs did have a family resemblance to the early post-war C1s. On the left is 4232 (UHA 232), a BMMO C3 with a Willowbrook C37C body dating from July 1954. This coach was rebodied in 1962 with a C36F Plaxton Panorama body and reclassified as a type CL3. In this form the coach's life was extended by some ten years. (M. A. Sutcliffe)

### 3308 (KHA 308)

Before Spencer House was built in Digbeth, between Rea Street and Mill Lane (in front of Digbeth garage), vehicles were parked on the waste ground. Parked on the rough ground is 3308 (KHA 308), a BMMO C1 with a Duple C30C body dating from April 1949. The bus was kept at Digbeth until 1954 and, after a brief two-year sojourn at Shrewsbury garage, spent the rest of its Midland Red career at Bearwood, from where it was operated as a dual-control trainer for six further years. Behind the coach are two unidentified SOS FEDDs and 3827 (NHA 827) – an almost new Brush-bodied BMMO B5B. Beyond the coach on the far side of Digbeth is the Horse & Groom Public House. (S. N. J. White)

## 3314 (KHA 314)

Standing in Stafford garage yard in 1961, in company with a two-door Austin A35 saloon, is 3314 (KHA 314). It looks a little dusty as it had spent the winter in store. As usual for all of the forty-five Duple C30C-bodied BMMO C1s, it had spent every winter in store from May 1949 when it entered service. It slumbered each year from late September until April before being prepared for its summer duties. 3314 (KHA 314), weighing some 6 tonnes 18¾ cwt, would stay in service until it was withdrawn in June 1965. (T. W. W. Knowles)

## 3320 (KHA 320)

Parked alongside Aberystwyth's railway station is Duple C30C bodied BMMO C1 3320 (KHA 320). At the rear is another C1. Sandwiched between them is one of the first batch of BMMO S15 dual-purpose single-deckers dating from 1957, which, during the summer peak when coach availability was at a premium, were pressed into service on excursion work. The Duple bodywork, with its sliding centre entrance door, was almost spot-on regarding its design, which was obviously derived from Midland Red's own specification and had evolved from the pre-war SLR and ONC designs, although the jazzy radiator grill looked as though it had come out of a Detroit factory. (A. N. Porter)

### 3326 (KHA 326)

On a day trip to Barry Island from the Birmingham area is Duple C30C-bodied 3326 (KHA 326). This underfloor-engined BMMO C1 had entered service in June 1949 and, for the first of its first five years, was based at Bearwood and Digbeth garages. In the days before motorways had been built, even the speedy C1s would have taken around six hours to get to Barry Island. It was taken out of service in 1965 but was converted to a dual-control driver training vehicle. It was reinstated in March 1966 at Bearwood depot, where it remained, until finally being taken out of service in September 1970. Parked behind is the 1939 Duple-bodied SOS ONC 2276 (FHA 408). Despite the latter coach having a front engine, the family resemblance between the Duple bodies on the two coaches, despite a ten-year difference in their ages, is noticeable. (S. N. J. White)

### 3327 (KHA 327)

Looking at first sight like a somewhat down-at-heel coach, the clue to 3327's (KHA 327) condition and use is the advertisement on the cantrail stating that 'Midland Red Require Drivers'. New in June 1949, it had latterly been allocated to Southgate Street garage, Leicester, before being withdrawn in June 1965 and converted to a dual-control driver training vehicle. It spent most of its driver training career at the Leicester garage and survived as the longest lived of all the BMMO C1s being finally retired in November 1976. (A. D. Broughall)

## 3329 (KHA329)

Parked in Derby bus station, near to the Trent Motor Services bus garage, is 3329 (KHA 329). This Duple-bodied BMMO C1 entered service in July 1949 from Sutton Coldfield garage. It remained at that garage until the spring of 1952 when it was transferred to Leamington Spa garage. The coach is in immaculate condition, although its size was becoming something of a restricting factor since the Construction & Use Regulation had allowed the length of single-deckers to be increased by 2 ½ feet and the width measurement by 6 inches. Thus, quite soon after their introduction, the C1s were competing with new coaches which were equipped with seven more seats. 3329 was withdrawn in July 1965. (P. Yeomans)

## 3333 (KHA 333)

Parked on the forecourt of Oldbury garage in 1949 is a brand new Duple C30C-bodied BMMO C1 coach 3333 (KHA 333). The C1s had a sliding central entrance passenger door and a recessed driver's windscreen – a feature particularly typical of buses in the West Midlands, which was designed to reduce reflections inside the driver's cab. 3333 spent the first two years of its life based at this garage which had opened on 12 April 1937. It also was the first Midland Red garage to be fitted with an automatic bus wash. Standing behind the coach is a second immaculately presented C1, in this case 3340 (KHA 340). With the centre door open, the style of flowered moquette, which was also used on the seat backs and squabs, is clearly visible. (D. R. Harvey Collection)

### 3338 (KHA 338)

Climbing up through Cheddar Gorge with its steep sides made of Jurassic limestone are two BMMO C1s. 3338 (KHA 338), along with 3304 (KHA 304) behind, are both on a day tour to Somerset and might well have come from the village of Cheddar at the bottom of the Gorge. There would have been time for a Midland Red organised afternoon tea and a quick trip around the tourist souvenir shops. There was also the opportunity to buy both the local Cheddar cheese and bottles of Somerset cider before embarking on their long journey home. The powerful BMMO horizontal 8.028-litre engine would have made light work of the climb out of Cheddar Gorge and, coupled to the four speed David Brown constant-mesh gearbox, would have made the driver's life quite easy ... especially if he did clutchless gear changes! (A. A. Cooper)

### 3342 (KHA 342)

This Duple-bodied BMMO C1 coach was taken out of service in 1961 along with 3308 and 3341, which were also withdrawn at the same time. 3342 (KHA 342) was converted to a dual-control trainer and was operated for the next five years from Bearwood garage's Driver Training School. It has just turned into St Margaret's bus station, in Leicester, in 1966, when recently allocated to Southgate Street garage, and is still wearing its red and black coach livery. It would continue in this role in January 1968. (A. D. Broughall)

## 3345 (KHA 345)

A batch of twelve coaches built as C26C by BMMO, between May and June 1950, were classified as the C2 class. They also had Duple bodywork, which superficially looked like the C1's, but they had C26C bodies and were intended for extended tours. These tours could last for up to two weeks and used specially selected high-class hotels. For their first two summers of touring, the C2s also had a courier to assist passengers. There were detailed differences which included an outward opening hinged central entrance door, a pair of recessed front windscreens as well as the omission of an external driver's door. The coaches were modernised in 1959 when their seating capacity was increased to thirty. At the same time, all twelve were externally modernised with large single front bumpers, a new, smaller radiator grill and extra chrome brightwork below the saloon windows and along the sides at floor level. This gave the frontal aspect a chunkier appearance, though whether this was an improvement on the original is open to question. They retained the red livery with a black roof, but the side mudguards were painted red. 3345 (KHA 345) is parked inside Digbeth coach station in 1964. (R. Marshall)

## 3346 (KHA 346)

Standing in Towyn, adjacent to Towyn Wharf station, on 31 August 1955, is 3346 (KHA 346), the second of the dozen BMMO C2s with Duple C26C bodywork. The twin recessed windscreens were a distinguishable feature of these coaches. It has been hired by the Talyllyn Railway Preservation Society for a visit to the narrow 2-foot 3-inch gauge railway. The Talyllyn Railway had opened as a mineral line in 1866 to transport slate, but due to years of decline and various quirks of fate it closed at the end of 1950. It was rescued by railway enthusiasts from the Birmingham area and it became the first railway in the world to be preserved as a heritage railway by volunteers. Hence the visit on a Midland Red coach some four years later. (K. Cope)

### 3346 (KHA 346)

Parked in Edgbaston Street after being rebodied is 3346 (KHA 346) again. This BMMO C2 was one of three to receive especially shortened Plaxton Embassy bodywork in 1962. These three coaches were then reclassified as CL2s. In this form, 3346 remained in service until the end of the 1970 season. When they were first delivered with their new bodies, the CL2s were painted all-over ivory white, but within a year they reverted to a red livery with black roofs. The coaches had Perspex cantrail windows while, very unusually, the main saloon windows all had small sliding ventilators. (D. R. Harvey Collection)

### 3348 (KHA 348)

En route to Weston-super-Mare and about to leave a refreshment stop in about 1960 is 3348 (KHA 348). Hopefully the driver will turn up soon as all his passengers are waiting for him. The C2 coach has its original un-rebuilt body with the original style of large C1-type radiator grill, albeit slightly disfigured and with split front bumpers. This coach received the Duple body from KHA 346 when that vehicle was rebodied by Plaxton in April 1963. Parked behind the C2 is an unidentified BMMO C5, also off on a day trip to Weston. (A. D. Broughall)

## 3350 (KHA 350)

3350 (KHA 350) one of the twelve Duple-bodied touring coaches of 1950, was one of three BMMO C2s to receive especially shortened Plaxton Embassy bodywork in 1962. 3350 returned to service in April 1962 and was reclassified CL2 by Midland Red. In their new form they also seated twenty-six passengers. It was decided not to lengthen the chassis at the rear on grounds of expense and, while the overall effect was distinctly more modern, their rebodied form rather looked like a Manx cat, i.e. tailless! When returned to service, they were painted in this bland all-over white livery with tiny silvered fleet names on the sides and front, which drew some criticism that resulted in them being repainted, in 1963, in the traditional red and black coaching colours of Midland Red. (J. Cockshott)

## 3351 (KHA 351)

Victoria coach station in Buckingham Palace Road was opened, in 1932, by London Coastal Coaches, a consortium of coach operators. The building is in a distinctive Art Deco style, and, when built, it had space for seventy-six coaches plus a large booking hall, shops, buffet, restaurant, lounge and bar. Travelling into the coach station in about 1960 is modernised BMMO C2 3351 (KHA 351). The coach has travelled from Birmingham by way of Coventry and Daventry on a journey that took five and a half hours. Following the Midland Red coach is a Bristol MW with a dual-purpose body and a Southdown Leyland Tiger Cub coach, while on the right is London Transport's RTW 119. (C. W. Routh)

## 3355 (KHA 355)

Being used on what Midland Red optimistically called a 'Scottish Cruise', an almost new 3355 (KHA 355) stands alongside Edinburgh's Waverley station on the wet stone set roadway. Towering over the station is the North British Hotel, adjacent at the corner between Princes Street and North Bridge, which had opened in 1902. The immaculately presented Duple C26C-bodied BMMO C2 was new in August 1950 and at this time was allocated to Bearwood garage. One of the distinguishing features of the C2's body, when compared to the slightly earlier C1s, was the lack of offside driver's cab door. For the 1954 touring season, 3355 was re-seated to C30C and was finally withdrawn in September 1965, after being in front-line service with the company for fifteen years – about one third longer than contemporary coaches. The advantage of these early post-war coaches was that their pioneering underfloor engine position enabled them to go from revolutionary in their youth, through a mid-life period when they still looked reasonably modern, to a final stateliness in old age. (S. N. J. White)

## 3356 (KHA 356)

Four of the Duple C26C-bodied always retained their original seating capacity and were chosen for renovation in 1959. These were 3345, 3351, 3354 and 3356. All were given new bumpers and smaller radiator grills that had a resemblance to designs fitted to cars being built by Austin at Longbridge. The twin recessed windscreens were retained as was the hinged opening centre entrance door. The last one, 3356 (KHA 356), is parked on the forecourt of Cheltenham coach station soon after having its mudguards painted red for the 1961 season. These modified C2s resumed work on coach cruises and despite their age were not withdrawn until 1966. (D. R. Harvey Collection)

# The Heavyweight Coaches of the Mid-1950s

In 1953 and 1954, more coaches were introduced and were the last ones built with a chassis. There were sixty-three C3 coaches and a further twelve C4 touring coaches built to the larger 30-foot long and 8-foot wide dimensions, with seating capacities of thirty-seven and thirty-two respectively. Weighing just over 7 ¼ tonnes and equipped with an up-rated version of the 8.028-litre BMMO KL engine, their progress was stately rather than sparkling. Despite that, they were solidly built, gave a very comfortable ride and were quite luxurious. These coaches further enhanced Midland Red's reputation amongst not only its loyal passenger following but also with their competing operators.

## 4179 (UHA 179)

Standing in a parking bay in Bournemouth when on tour is 4179 (UHA 179). This was the first of the sixty-three Willowbrook C37C-bodied BMMO C3 coaches. This coach entered service in April 1954 and would remain in service until its withdrawal in July 1965. They were fitted with the horizontal version of new BMMO KL 8.028-litre engine but had a modified version of the S13 dual-purpose single-deckers. They were fitted with a five-speed overdrive gearbox and weighed 7 tonnes 5 ½ cwt. The bodies were Midland Red's first single-deckers built to the still fairly new 30-foot long dimensions. (Vectis Transport)

## 4180 (UHA 180)

Leaving the Mill Lane exit of Digbeth coach station is a rather dirty-looking Willowbrook-bodied 4180 (UHA 180). It is being driven by a mechanic, suggesting that it is going round-the-block to re-enter the garage section of the coach station, where the bus washing facilities and engineering pits were located. Here the coach would be checked over and spruced up for its next tour of duty. 4180 was placed into service in April 1954 from Digbeth, where it stayed for just two years before passing for the rest of its career to Hinckley garage. It was one of the last of the un-rebuilt C3s to remain in service and was not withdrawn until November 1966. (R. Hannay)

## 4185 (UHA 185)

4185 (UHA 185) is parked outside the entrance to the Midland Red Cleveland Road garage in Wolverhampton. Alongside and behind the coach is the Atkinson breweries-owned Queen's Arms. The half-full Willowbrook-bodied BMMO C3 was one of the Loughborough company's underfloor coach designs, similar ones being operated by Black & White but mounted on Guy Arab LUF chassis. The coach bodies were fitted out to Midland Red's strict specification with their own fixtures and fittings. 4185 entered service in May 1954 and was therefore still fairly new when about to leave for the fairly short run to Digbeth coach station in Birmingham. (S. N. J. White)

## 4190 (UHA 190)

Driving through St Margaret's bus station is 4190 (UHA 190). Demoted to a dual-purpose vehicle with the fitting of a front destination box, this Plaxton-rebodied BMMO CL3 was taken out of service in October 1961 when it was sent to Scarborough to be fitted with a C36F Panorama style body. It re-entered service in April 1962. The new bodies were 31 feet 8 inches long and so the C3 chassis was extended at the rear to support this extra length. In all, some seventeen C3s were rebodied by Plaxton and in this form lasted until 1971. A similar Plaxton body mounted on a Leyland Leopard PSU3 chassis, owned by Black & White Motorways of Cheltenham, is parked on the left. (D. R. Harvey Collection)

## 4193 (UHA 193)

When new, the Plaxton Panorama rebodied BMMO CL3s were delivered in an unrelieved all-over white livery. This rather presaged the similar National Bus Company coach livery introduced in 1972, which was not popular with the public. On the rebodied CL3s, the white wore badly and quickly looked scruffy, and with only tiny chromed 'Midland Red' lettering to identify the owner, the bland and anonymous appearance was not in keeping with Midland Red's philosophy of a luxury touring coach. As a result, after just one summer season the coaches were all repainted in an all-over red with a black roof livery, although a variation of this did include a white band below the windscreen and saloon windows. 4193 (UHA 193) is parked on the entrance forecourt to Bearwood garage soon after being rebodied and still retains the original one-piece windscreen. This was soon replaced on all these rebodies with a two-piece windscreen with a central dividing strip. His was done in order to keep expenses down in the event of a broken windscreen. One of the advertising hoardings reads 'THE FRIENDLY MIDLAND RED INVITES YOU TO INSPECT THE NEW LUXURY COACH TO BE EMPLOYED ON MIDLAND RED CRUISES DURING THE 1962 SEASON'. (A. D. Broughall)

## 4200 (UHA 200)

Entering service in June 1954 and being withdrawn in September 1965, 4200 (UHA 200) led a fairly quiet life as it was allocated to Oldbury garage for its entire operational career. This BMMO C3 is parked in Victoria coach station, London, alongside the newer BMMO CM5. While the heavyweight C3 could not achieve the same speeds on the motorways as the newer coach, it could give a comfortable and stately ride down the M1. 4200 was one of several C3s to be given a new chromed radiator grill, which had fewer horizontal bars (taking its cue from the earlier C2s) but lacked the subtly of the original design. (D. R. Harvey Collection)

## 4201 (UHA 201)

The BMMO C3s were used on a variety of coaching activities. These coaches could be found working on long-distance work as well as excursions and day trips. Standing in Northampton's bus station on its way back to Coventry is a well-patronised 4201 (UHA 201), with an ECW-bodied Royal Blue Bristol LS6B and a camel-backed luggage roof rack behind it. Compared to the Royal Blue coach, the Willowbrook body looks a real heavyweight structure and even after being built some seventeen years later, the C3's body did have design echoes of the 1937 English Electric design. (R. F. Mack)

## 4212 (UHA 212)

Leaving Cheltenham's coach station on a hot summer's day is BMMO C3 4212 (UHA 212). This Willowbrook-bodied thirty-seven-seater is carrying a full load as it begins its journey back to Birmingham on a journey that would take two hours forty minutes. Alongside the Midland Red is NDG 160, one of Black & White's Guy Arab LUFs with a Duple C37C body also dating from 1954. The Black & White-owned coach, with all its extra chrome embellishments, somehow does look as refined as the much plainer liveried Midland Red. (D. R. Harvey Collection)

## 4214 (UHA 214)

Speeding into the iconic Royal Blue Art Deco coach and bus station, at the Square in Bournemouth, is 4214 (UHA 214). This BMMO C3's Willowbrook C37C body positively sparkles in the summer sunshine in the early 1960s. The coach is on an excursion to the south coast and, despite being at least six years old, still retains the red and black livery with gold lining out. The journey on this Associated Motorways service from Birmingham took all day. It left Digbeth at 9.30 a.m. and arrived at the resort at 6.05 p.m. with a five-minute layover at Banbury, Gloucester Green, Oxford, Newbury and Winchester; exhausting to the extent that one needed a holiday to recover from the journey. (D. R. Harvey Collection)

## 4220 (UHA 220)

Parked outside the Imperial Hotel in St George's Place, Liverpool, on 26 May 1963 is 4220 (UHA 220). Behind it and the Hillman Minx series saloon is the large Co-op department store. The 1954 chassis of the BMMO C3 was rebodied over the winter of 1961–62 with a Plaxton Panorama C36F body and re-entered service in April 1962 as a CL3-type painted in an all-over white livery, which looked quite awful. For the next season, along with the other C3Ls, 4220 was repainted in almost traditional Midland Red coaching colours, with the majority of its lower body being painted red and the roof black. The only remnant of the 1962 season's livery that was retained was the thin strip of white below the windscreen and saloon windows. In its first year in service, the attractive but expensive single piece windscreen was replaced by a two-piece unit, which in the event of an accident was much cheaper to repair. (G. Pattison)

## 4228 (UHA 228)

Leaving High Town, Bewdley, via New Road, on a half-day tour to the Severn Valley area, is 4228 (UHA 228). This Willowbrook C37C-bodied BMMO C3 was new in July 1954 and when on this tour was allocated to Wellington garage. High Town was where the larger hotels and public houses were located, as well as the main shopping area for the town, with the added attraction of the Georgian buildings and the raised half-timbered Bridgnorth Town Hall, dating from 1650, standing in the middle of High Street. The driver must have been pleased that he was going downhill towards the River Severn and Bewdley's Low Town, as the hill was a steep climb and would have required a double-declutch gear change into first gear. He would 'have to hold his mouth right!' 4228 was withdrawn in April 1966 after twelve years' service with Midland Red. (R. F. Mack)

## 4230 (UHA 230)

The advantage of having some of the BMMO C3s rebodied was that the Plaxton Panorama body gave the vehicle a much more modern appearance and a wide front entrance door controlled by the driver. After eight years with its original body, the new Plaxton body was fitted in early 1962 as type CL3 and allocated to Leamington garage. 4230 (UHA 230) was one of the seventeen C3 chassis to be chosen to be rebodied. It is on a Scottish tour to Ayrshire and Galloway and is in the short-lived all-over white livery, which it only retained in its first year back in service. It still has its original one-piece windscreen. Behind the coach is a partially hidden Morris Minor 1000, a Riley 1.5 and a Ford Anglia, all of which are being overtaken by a Volkswagen Beetle that is registered in Ayrshire in May 1962. (G. Stainthorpe)

## 4231 (UHA 231)

Fort William railway station was built in stone by the West Highland Railway and featured a turret and a double-arched entrance, in front of which CL3 coach 4231 (UHA 231) is parked. It closed on 9 June 1975 and was demolished immediately afterwards to permit construction of the Fort William bypass. 4231 is in the summer 1963 livery of red and black and has just a small white band below only the saloon windows. By now the coach has acquired a two-piece windscreen with a central dividing strip, which was cheaper to replace than the vastly more expensive single unit. These long coach cruises, such as to Devon and Cornwall, the Lake District or, as in this case, the Scottish Highlands, were the prime reason for rebodying these 1954 vintage chassis, as the BMMO C4 touring coaches were getting a bit long in the tooth! As a result, 4231 was used in this capacity until it was withdrawn in May 1971. Even then, and unusually for a Midland Red chassis, it was sold to a Rowley Regis operator, who ran it for two years, before being sold on to London operators where it survived until September 1974. (A. J. Douglas)

## 4238 (UHA 238)

Parked in Northumberland Avenue facing Trafalgar Square, with Embankment station in the distance, is 4238 (UHA 238) – a Willowbrook-bodied BMMO C3. Behind the coach is a Vauxhall Wyvern EIX car and an Austin A35 saloon beyond that. The coach is standing outside one of the many luxury hotels lining Northumberland Avenue and is working on a private hire duty in about 1959, when the coach was only about five years old. It was new in September 1954 and entered service in the following April. This coach was usually allocated to either Southgate Street in Leicester or Nuneaton garage and would remain in service until October 1965. (M. Rooum)

## 4242 (UHA 242)

One could be forgiven for assuming that the body on the prototype C4 touring coach had been built by Willowbrook, who had constructed the original bodies on the C3 coaches. In reality, the body on 4242 (UHA 242) was constructed by Carlyle, Midland Red's name for their own coachwork, with a C32C body. It entered service in May 1954 and, until its withdrawal in March 1966, it spent its time allocated briefly to Bearwood garage. For its last eight years it was based at Digbeth. Early in its career it is parked outside the prestigious Norfolk Hotel in Hagley Road, Birmingham, only about 2 miles away from its then Bearwood garage base. Parked behind it is a rather splendid Standard Vanguard four-door saloon. (D. R. Harvey Collection)

## 4243 (UHA 243)

The production batch of eleven C4 coaches built as C32C had bodies supplied by Alexander, who at that time were very much a supplier of bodies to Scottish operators. The Alexander bodies were an almost exact replica of the body built by Carlyle and, along with some double-deck bodies which were for war-time Daimler CWA6 chassis for West Bromwich Corporation, the C4 coaches were among Alexander's first forays into the English bus market. To the left of the coach is BR 2-10-0 9F Crosti-boilered No. 92025, which was one of ten; all of which were initially allocated to Saltley Motive Power Depot. (R. F. Mack)

## 4247 (UHA 247)

In original condition on a Midland Red Coach Cruise is 4247 (UHA 247), still sporting its original narrow-slatted radiator grill. These BMMO C4s had an Alexander C32C body which was a remarkable copy of the Willowbrook bodies on the C3 coaches. A distinguished feature of their touring-style bodies were the cant rail windows but otherwise they looked very similar to the C3s. The C4s weighed 7 tonnes 7 cwt, which was slightly more than the C3 with the increase being accounted for by the more luxurious interior body fittings. It had entered service in June 1954 and, although re-seated in March 1959 to a C37C seating layout, it continued in service until withdrawal finally took place in October 1966. (D. R. Harvey Collection)

## 4249 (UHA 249)

Entering Rigby Road bus and coach station in Blackpool is 4249 (UHA 249), when working on an excursion to the world-famous seaside resort. This BMMO C4 touring coach had an Alexander C32C body and was new in 1954. The coach, fitted with curved glass quarter light cantrail windows, has been fitted with the later radiator grill. Behind the coach is a Northern Counties-bodied Guy Arab IV. The tram tracks on the left lead to Blackpool Corporation's tram depot. (R. F. Mack)

## 4253 (UHA 253)

Parked outside an immaculately clean-fronted prestigious hotel in Torquay, on a Devon and Cornwall coach cruise in about 1955, is 4253 (UHA 253) – a BMMO C4 with an Alexander C32C body. The coach cruises to the South West were for either seven or ten days and meals and high-quality hotels were all part of the all-inclusive cost. The reduction (by five) in the seating capacity, when compared to the C3, gave the passengers considerably more leg room, while the four curved quarter lights on each side of the cant rail (clearly visible) enhanced the luxurious specification of these coaches for the extended tour work. By way of contrast to the almost new coach, a 1936 Standard Nine two door saloon is parked in front of 4253. (W. S. Godden)

# Motorway Express Coaches

The need for faster coaches really reared its head when the Government announced that a new motorway would be opened between London and Birmingham. The new Midland Red motorway service left Birmingham and proceeded via the A45 to Coventry and then along the new M45 to meet the M1 at Junction 17. The service was first introduced by Midland Red on 2 November 1959, with the first Midland Red motorway express coach getting onto the M45 at Dunchurch – the motorway's most northern point of access to the A45 – just half an hour after the M1 motorway had opened. The new coaches designed for this service were the BMMO CM5Ts, which could cruise at 80 mph in comfort that was previously unheard of in even recently built coaches. The motorway coaches especially did not have very long lives, having been subjected to a life of barely six years hammering up and down the M45, M1 and M5 motorways.

## 4722 (722 BHA)

Waiting to load up with passengers going to Birmingham via Aylesbury, 4722 (722 BHA) will soon return north from the London terminus at Victoria coach station. 4722 (722 BHA) was intended to be the last of the S14 single-deckers but was turned out as the first of the coaches, some of which became famous as the motorway express coaches. The original frontal design was added to what was essentially an S14 body frame and included a two-piece rounded windscreen, single-blind destination box, new grill design and an outward opening passenger door that was located ahead of the front axle for the first time on a BMMO coach design. The coach was fitted with a BMMO 8.028-litre diesel engine with a CAV turbocharger, producing 98 bhp at 1750 rpm. It had a four-speed gearbox and twin rear wheels. It was also fitted with disc brakes on the front and rear wheels. This coach was easily identified by the rather odd arrangement of windows at the rear and the twin windows on the rear offside, one of which housed the emergency door. (J. C. Cockshott)

## 4722 (722 BHA)

As well as being used on the new M1 motorway services, 4722 (722 BHA) was also used on other coach services. In this case, on a miserable-looking day, it is going to the coach station in Cheltenham on an Associated Motorways connecting service. The small pair of rear saloon windows was an untidy feature of this prototype and enabled the coach to be easily recognisable. 4722 was completed on 1 April 1958 and was well appointed with forced ventilation, full length luggage racks, extensive use of fibre-glass sound proofing, while all the side panels are made of the same material. The roof was made in one moulded piece and all of these features enabled the unladen weight to be less than 6.5 tonnes. It was finally withdrawn in 1971. (D. R. Harvey Collection)

## 4774 (774 GHA)

Travelling along Corporation Street, and about to pass Lower Priory in Birmingham's city centre, is the unmarked and anonymous 4774 (774 GHA), being road tested during August 1958. One might have thought that the powers that be at Carlyle Road Works might have chosen a less public route on which to road test the first of their new coaches. This was the first coach in the initial first production batch of twenty-four vehicles numbered 4774–4797 (774–797 GHA). These were delivered in 1958 and featured a new Dutch lantern-styled windscreen, designed to reduce reflections from the saloon at night. 4774 was the first of the C5s to be withdrawn in February 1970. (L. Mason)

## 4776 (776 GHA)

Parked in a side road near to Rugby public school, 4776 (776 GHA) is a standard BMMO C5 coach and has the standard, rather tasteful, livery of red bodywork with black roof. It had entered service on 1 November 1958 as type C5 and spent most of its life as a coach allocated to Digbeth. 4776 was downgraded to a dual-purpose bus reclassified in September 1966 as type C5A and was fitted out for one-man operation in January 1970. (Milepost)

## 4780 (780 GHA)

Looking splendid when attending the Showbus Rally at Duxford on 26 September 2010, 4780 had only been fully restored just twelve months earlier. It is parked in front of the amazing American Air Museum. 4780 (780 GHA) was new on 25 March 1959 as type C5, which was the standard version of the C5 coach with four-speed manual gearboxes and the normally aspirated version of the BMMO 8.028-litre engine. It was withdrawn in January 1971 and was sold as a mobile caravan in Dudley, where it survived until bought for preservation in June 1998. (D. R. Harvey)

## 4783 (783 GHA)

Travelling along the Promenade, in Margate, with a full load of passengers, on 23 July 1960, is 4783 (783 GHA), one of the initial batch of BMMO C5s with Carlyle C37F bodywork. These were intended for excursion and touring duties and gradually replaced the 1954-built C3s and C4s which were becoming to look their age. 4783 entered service from Oldbury garage in April 1959 and, like many of these coaches, once their seating capacity began to fall short of the capacity of 36-foot-long coaches operated by other companies, the writing was on the wall for the C5s, and they were demoted to basically mundane bus work, becoming Midland Red C5As from 1966 until withdrawal in late 1970. (P. Redmond)

## 4802 (802 HHA)

The second of the eleven examples of the BMMO CM5T turbo-charged motorway express coaches was 4802 (802 HHA). This had a C34FT layout with a toilet and had a five-speed overdrive constant mesh. New on 1 November 1959, it was eventually converted to the CS5 specification. 4802 has just left Digbeth coach station in 1960 as it starts on the motorway express service to London. It is passing the impressive Digbeth Civic Hall, which was opened with a seating capacity of 2,000 on 16 January 1908. The M1's first section was opened on 1 November 1959 between Junction 18, at Crick, near Rugby, to Junction 5, at Watford. On its completion in 1966, the M1 acted as a fast link road between London and Birmingham, but the halcyon days of the CM5T coaches were already over! 4802 was converted to type C5A and was finally withdrawn in April 1971. (L. Mason)

## 4803 (803 HHA)

As 4803 (HHA 803) leaves Digbeth coach station in Birmingham from the Mill Lane exit and turns right into Digbeth, it is actually not leaving to go to London. It is empty and is in reality just going around the block to go round to the entrance of the coach station in Rea Street, where it will refuel before pulling down to the loading point at the Mill Lane exit. This BMMO CM5T shows off its nearside rear toilet area behind the frosted glass windows. The toilet space reduced the seating capacity of the coach by three, making it a thirty-four-seater. (R. F. Mack)

## 4809 (809 HHA)

The structural integrity of the Carlyle-built coach bodies on the BMMO CM5Ts was put to the test when 4809 (809 HHA) overturned when travelling south on the M1, some 2 miles north of Newport Pagnell Services, after skidding during a torrential rain storm when trying to avoid a car which had pulled out into the outside lane in front of 4809. The body was built on Metal Section frames that were made in Oldbury; these structures were well-known for their rigidity and longevity and, as a result, only three passengers were slightly injured. The damage to 4809 was restricted to only a few dented panels and the nearside of the roof and the bus made its own way back to its garage under its own power. (D. R. Harvey Collection)

## 4811 (811 HHA)

Speeding along the M1 motorway, on the express service from Birmingham to London, is BMMO CM5T motorway coach 4811 (811 HHA). The service was first introduced by Midland Red on 2 November 1959 with the first Midland Red motorway express coach getting onto the M45 at Dunchurch – the motorway's most northern point of access to the A45 – just half an hour after the motorway M1 had opened. Midland Red had introduced its first non-stop motorway express coach in the UK from Birmingham to London. The age of fast coach travel had arrived as it took only fifty-nine minutes to travel 65 miles to St Albans. The complete trip of 117 miles, from Digbeth to the Victoria coach-station, was made in two hours and fifty-one minutes. This was thirty-four minutes ahead of schedule and almost half the time of the company's long-established London–Birmingham routes. Speeds of up to 90 mph were regularly recorded before speed limits were imposed and the turbocharged CM5Ts were capable of the 'magic tonne' in service. 4811 (811 HHA) entered service in July 1960 and was used for five years on this arduous coach service. (D. R. Harvey Collection)

## 4813 (813 HHA)

The BMMO CM5 turbo-charged motorway express coach had a five-speed overdrive constant mesh gearbox but lacked a toilet compartment. This increased its seating capacity to C37F. Only seven such coaches were built, specifically 4800, 4805–4808, 4812 and 4813, and were used for the shorter motorway service where a toilet was deemed unnecessary. They had the same colour layout in the saloon with a peony and white scheme, with a simulated leopard skin moquette for the coach seat covers. The last of these seven, 4813 (813 HHA), is in Victoria coach station having worked on the shorter motorway service from Coventry. It is fitted with the suitable roof-mounted 'COVENTRY–LONDON MOTORWAY EXPRESS SLIP BOARD'. (D. R. Harvey Collection)

## 4814 (814 HHA)

Under construction at Carlyle Road Works in the spring of 1960 is the future 4814 (814 BHA). The coach can be identified by the fleet number being chalked on the radiator. The front and rear sections of the coach are being fabricated onto the central S14 bus type body saloon. The BMMO CM5T had a C34FT layout and continued with this arrangement until 1966. When the larger BMMO CM6T motorway-coaches were introduced in February 1965, and forty-nine Leyland Leopard type C7 coaches later the same year, many of the BMMO C5 coaches were downgraded and adapted for bus work. This C5A conversion work was carried out on forty-five vehicles by BMMO, at Central Works in Edgbaston, beginning with 4804 (804 HHA) in 1966. In 1970, 4814 was finally withdrawn having been used as a service bus for almost one year. (L. Mason)

## 4819 (819 HHA)

Being prepared for a bus rally on 26 March 2000 is 4819 (819 HHA). This was one of the twenty-two examples produced as standard C37F BMMO C5 coaches and was beautifully preserved. New in April 1961, it was finally withdrawn in January 1971. Its subsequent career was more interesting than its operational one. After withdrawal, it immediately was sold to the Lichfield Speedway Supporters Club before being sold for preservation in 1983. After that, it went through the hands of no less than four preservation groups. Behind the C5 is the author's ex-Birmingham City Transport Crossley-bodied Crossley 2489 (JOJ 489). (D. R. Harvey)

## 4826 (826 HHA)

4826 (826 HHA) has just left the Busy Bee layover stop on the A45 as it travels towards Birmingham on the M1 motorway express service. This coach was one of the thirty-four BMMO CM5T turbo-charged motorway express coaches that were fitted with toilets. Despite the main saloon section of the coach being based on the S14 bus frame, the coach was well disguised, especially at the front, with the unique Dutch-style lantern windscreen, designed to cut back on the amount of reflection from the saloon at night. The front passenger door was manually operated and, once inside the saloon, the deep seats, with their own individual adjustable headrests and side panels, were finished in multi-coloured floral moquette. 4826 was one of the CM5Ts to be converted to type CS5. This involved various engine modifications to increase performance without resorting to the expense of fitting a turbocharger. This enabled the CS6s to continue to run on the motorway express services if required. (R. F. Mack)

## 4834 (834 HHA)

By now downgraded to a type C5A, many of the BMMO C5 coaches were adapted for bus work. This conversion involved fitting revised bus-type destination gear, converting the passenger door to power-operation opening inwards and removing the turbocharger and the toilet. Thus, converted to a coach-seated bus, the vehicles received overall red BMMO bus livery, which did look rather drab. 4834 (834 HHA) entered service in August 1961 and is standing in the approach to Wolverhampton High Level station when working on the one-and-a-quarter-hour-long 885 service via Wombourn, Kingswinford, Stourbridge and Hagley back to its home base in Kidderminster. It was fitted for O-M-O in May 1970 and was withdrawn in February 1971. (D. R. Harvey Collection)

# Going 36 Feet Long

The success of the CM5Ts on their pioneering and highly successful operation on the M1 service, between Birmingham and London, proved to be their Achilles Heel, as within a few years they were obviously lacking the seating capacity when compared to other operators, who had introduced the new 36-foot-long by 8-foot 2.5-inch-wide construction and use dimensions introduced in 1961. The irony was that Midland Red had played a key part in getting this new legislation passed into law but had only pioneered single-deck buses. As other large coach operators began to introduce 36-foot-long coaches, Midland Red had to get back to the top of the league again, and in 1962 BMMO produced a prototype CM6 vehicle. The Metal Sections body framework was based on the BMMO S17 buses and had six bays with fixed windows and forced ventilation. The first of the twenty-nine CM6 coaches were introduced in 1965. For six years the CM6s were used on the majority of the company's high-speed motorway services. This was until they were replaced by Leyland Leopards with Plaxton coach bodies, but without the advantage of having toilet facilities.

## 5295 (5495 HA)

The prototype 36-foot-long CM6T was completed on 12 September 1962 and, after a considerable amount of road testing, it entered service at Digbeth garage with the experimental department on the 15 March 1963 as 5295 (5495 HA). They monitored the progress of the coach for its first two years of service and ran alongside the BMMO CM5TS. The new coach was fitted with a BMMO 10.5-litre naturally aspirated engine, which, after a few months in service with a five-speed manual overdrive gearbox, was re-equipped with an SCG five-speed semi-automatic with a direct-drive fifth ratio. The basic body structure was based on the BMMO S17, suitably fitted out for motorway duties with forty-six coach seats and forced ventilation. It is parked in Digbeth coach station when still sporting its original lantern-style windscreen à la the CM5s. Ironically this style was removed, and a new curved version was fitted. (L. Mason)

## 5295 (5495 HA)

Loading up with passengers in Pool Meadow bus station, Coventry, before leaving for London via the M1 is 5295 (5495 HA). It is sporting the new curved windscreen which was very similar to the original one fitted initially to the C5 prototype 4722! This windscreen became the standard for the CM6Ts and replaced the Dutch lantern style one which it was built with that had looked like that sported by 4809 (809 HHA) to the rear. The seating capacity had by now been reduced by two to a C44FT layout. By 1965, after it had been taken out of the control of the Carlyle Road experimental shop department, 5295 was allocated to Rugby garage and was used extensively on this Coventry to London motorway express service. The coach was always presented in Midland Red's red with a black roof livery, which had begun in the early 1930s with the ill-fated SOS XL coaches, and which would be retained until the introduction of the awful all-over white livery of the National Bus Company's coaches. 5295 was finally withdrawn in March 1973. (D. R. Harvey Collection)

## 5646 (BHA 646C)

The first of the production BMMO CM6Ts was 5646 (BHA 646C), which entered service on 1 March 1965. Throughout its six-and-a-half-year service life, 5646 was allocated to Bearwood garage for use pounding up and down the M1 on the motorway express service to London. The coach is travelling along Coventry Road in Sheldon, Birmingham, and from the rear clearly shows the position of the toilet compartment behind the frosted glazing on the nearside rear corner. The toilet facilities on these longer coaches benefitted with the slightly wider 8-foot 2.5-inch bodywork. Being an underfloor vehicle, the coach boasted a cavernous rear luggage area behind the large twin rear boot doors. (L. Mason)

## 5649 (BHA 649C)

About to turn into Victoria coach station, on 17 July 1965, is a Carlyle-bodied BMMO CM6T. This fully laden coach was barely three months old as it completes its journey from Birmingham. With their 10.45-litre naturally aspirated BMMO KL engine and a SCG five-speed semi-automatic gearbox, they were able run continuously on the motorway express service at speeds in excess of 85 mph. They had front and rear discs brakes. Noticeable is the amount of chrome-plated script above and on the front grill. This coach was repainted in January 1968 into the later red with maroon roof coach livery and was withdrawn in July 1972, before being broken up by Hudley of Wednesbury during the following month. (Photofives)

## 5652 (BHA 652C)

Enhanced by the ribbed aluminium strips, a bus-type destination box and an all-over NBC white coach livery, about one year before it was due to be withdrawn. 5652 (BHA 652C) stands in Victoria coach station. Mechanically, despite its age, the coach was still capable of high speed motorway work, but the bodies were becoming in need of heavy remedial work. Twenty-four of these vehicles were built as BMMO CM6Ts with forty-four seats and rear toilet. The legal lettering, despite the NBC livery, still stated that the coach was owned by the Birmingham & Midland Company. 5652 was one of the last to be taken out of service. (D. R. Harvey Collection)

### 5656 (BHA 656C)

Preserved in the Midland Red all-over red livery is 5656 (BHA 656C), at the Showbus Rally at Duxford on 26 September 2010. It is parked in front of the American Air Museum. 5656 entered service in September 1965 and by August 1972 was in service with this livery, having gone through the black roof phase when it was new, and the maroon roof period for five years from September 1967. It was withdrawn in September 1974 and eventually passed to BaMMOT, Wythall, in May 1978 for preservation. (D. R. Harvey)

### 5663 (DHA 963C)

5663 (DHA 963C), another of the BMMO CM6Ts with Carlyle C44T bodywork, leaves Pool Meadow bus station in Coventry on its way to London. The coach had arrived from Nuneaton, where it was garaged from its delivery in December 1965 for all but a few months of its service life. The CM6Ts all suffered from corrosion problems as they ran on the gritted motorways throughout the winter months and had never received any anti-corrosion treatment to the sub-frames and the underbody. (A. J. Douglas)

## 5668 (EHA 668D)

There were five BMMO CM6 coaches and they were built as C46F. They wore the usual red and black BMMO coach livery and were noticeable for their lack of a toilet. 5668 (EHA 668D) was new in March 1966 and was allocated to Worcester garage. It is crossing Smallbrook Ringway, in Birmingham, on its way to the Station Street terminus of the newly introduced X44 service to Worcester. The M5 motorway opened on Friday 20 July 1962, when Midland Red started operation of new motorway express service X44, running an hourly service between Birmingham, Selly Oak and Worcester. The former 144 service via the A38 route had a journey time of ninety-three minutes, whereas the new X44 service reduced the time down to fifty minutes. This was faster than the contemporary scheduled railway time. 5668 (EHA 668D) was withdrawn in April 1974. (D. R. Harvey Collection)

# The Leyland Leopard Era

All the subsequent coaches bought and operated by Midland Red after 1966 were built on the Leyland Leopard chassis. Financial restrictions and the steady loss of the skilled work force at Carlyle Road Works meant that specialist coach designs based on in-house-built chassis were just too expensive to construct. Of the two alternatives available, namely the AEC Reliance and the Leyland Leopard, the cheaper and less sophisticated Leyland Motors Model was purchased, becoming the standard coach chassis in the fleet. From 1965 until 1981 Midland Red purchased no less than 281 coaches from Leyland Motors with the addition of a solitary Leyland Tiger. They had bodies built by Duple and latterly Willowbrook but the most popular choice by far were those constructed by Plaxtons of Scarborough, who supplied 201 units.

## 5779 (CHA 79C)
Travelling up Trinity Street in Coventry is 5779 (CHA 79C). It is still sparklingly new and looks immaculate when on its way to Llandudno on a day trip. With the roof ventilators lifted up, it looks as if the weather might be good for the excursion. This batch of forty-nine Leyland Leopard PSU3/4R coaches, which were classified LC7 by Midland Red and represented 5779, was new in July 1965. 5779 spent the majority of its working life being allocated to Digbeth garage. It was withdrawn by Midland Red in February 1976 whereupon it passed to National Travel South West for another year's service. (A. A. Cooper)

## 5790 (CHA 90C)
About to leave Great Yarmouth coach station is Duple Commander C49F-bodied 5790 (CHA 90C). This was one of the forty-nine Duple C49F-bodied Leyland Leopard PSU3/4Rs delivered in August 1965 to Bearwood garage. It spent its last years at Evesham and Hinckley garages before being withdrawn in March 1976 after nearly eleven years of service. It is wearing the all-white corporate livery of the National Bus Company, which made it look like every other coach in that operator's fleet. The only clue to its real ownership was the 'MIDLAND RED' fleet name on the side of the coach. (C. D. Mann)

## 5797 (CHA 97C)
Standing in Shrewsbury bus station on 15 June 1969, with a group of rather bored looking elderly ladies, is 5797 (CHA 97C). This Leyland Leopard PSU3/4R had a Duple C49F body. It entered service in August 1965 and was allocated to Digbeth garage for the whole of its eleven years in service. There were forty-nine of these Leyland Leopard PSU3/4R with Duple C49F bodywork. They were equipped with pneumocyclic transmission, air brakes and the Leyland horizontal version of the 9.8-litre 0600 engine. 5798 was new in September 1965. It is in the all-over red livery with a maroon roof. After withdrawal by Midland Red, it passed briefly to NBC for another seven months, being finally withdrawn in October 1976. (G. Pattison)

## 5811 (CHA 111C)

Leaving Cheltenham coach station on a connecting service is 5811 (CHA 111C). This Leyland Leopard PSU3/4R entered service in October 1965 and had a 36-foot-long Duple C49F bodywork. If slightly underpowered with their 9.8-litre horizontal version of the Leyland 0600 engine, as far as the driver was concerned their pneumocyclic gearboxes and air brakes were a real boon. It looks extremely smart in the Midland Red coach livery of red with black roof. (D. R. Harvey Collection)

## 5818 (CHA 818C)

On a very wet day, Duple-bodied Leyland Leopard PSU3/4R 5818 (CHA 818C) splashes its way through Norwich on its way to a stoical day out in Great Yarmouth. The class were numbered 5774–5822 and were classified as the LC7-type by the company. The Duple Commander 36-foot-long C49F body looks extremely stately in its traditional red with a black roof livery, which never seemed to age. These coaches were particularly long-lived, some being sold and converted to dual-purpose vehicles fitted with front destination boxes on the roof. (D. F. Parker)

## 5823 (CHA 123C)

The solitary LC8 was 5823 (CHA 123C). It was purchased for use on extended coach tours and entered service in July 1965. It had a 30-foot-long Plaxton Panorama C36F body with a low-mounted mouth-like radiator grill, which was mounted on a Leyland Leopard L2T chassis. As it was for cruising, this solitary coach, classified LC8, had a Leyland 0600 engine, a synchromesh manual gearbox with an Eaton two-speed rear axle. It is parked at the back of Digbeth garage yard in company with a Vauxhall Victor saloon. It was repainted in NBC white coach livery in April 1974. After its withdrawal it was sold to Leeds City Council Education Dept, who operated it for another eight years. It was finally withdrawn at the end of 1984. (D. R. Harvey)

## 5827 (GHA 327D)

A further fifteen Leyland Leopard PSU4/4Rs with Leyland 0600 engines and with Plaxton Panorama C36F 30-foot 10-inch long bodies entered service during 1966 as 5824–5838 (CHA 324–338D). They were built for extended coach duties and were classified type LC9 by Midland Red. Standing in a coach park in Nottingham in company with Barton's 898 is 5827 (GHA 327D). These coaches saw off the BMMO C3s and represented a smarter-looking coach for the 1960s. With a goodly amount of chrome bodywork corrugated strips around the front of the body, 5827 had entered service in July 1966 from Sandacre Street garage and was later variously allocated to Wigston and Southgate Street garages, all in the Leicester area. A real 'Ay up me duck' coach! It was withdrawn in November 1976 and by January 1978 it emerged as a conversion to a recovery vehicle. It passed to Midland Red (South) Ltd, Rugby, at formation, on 6 September 1981, and was usually allocated to Leamington depot. It was withdrawn in May 2002 and was bought for preservation during the following year. (D. R. Harvey Collection)

### 5830 (GHA 330D)

Waiting for its next recovery mission in Leamington garage yard in January 1988 is 5830 (GHA 330D). This Plaxton-bodied Leyland Leopard PSU3/4R entered service in July 1966. It was converted to a recovery vehicle in February 1980 with a single bay crew compartment and an open rear platform cut off immediately behind the rear axle. The accommodation for the travelling mechanics still retained the remnants of the luxury that the coach originally had. Some of these conversions became their garage's pet vehicle and the crew compartment was kept in immaculate condition. 5830 variously ran on the 092 AC trade plate before being re-registered permanently as Q341 GVC, which it is carrying here. (D. R. Harvey)

### 5833 (GHA 333D)

Parked in Victoria coach station, having just arrived in London, is Plaxton-bodied Leyland Leopard PSU3/4R 5833 (GHA 333D) which is standing alongside a Southdown coach. New in August 1966, initially it was allocated to Oldbury garage before beginning a somewhat nomadic life, including periods at Bromsgrove, Evesham, Leicester Sandacre Street and Banbury garages. It was beautifully presented in the coach livery of red with a black roof. Withdrawn in December 1976, it was subsequently passed to Astonnes Coaches, Kempsey, as a C45F vehicle, and then to Everton Coaches, Droitwich. (D. R. Harvey Collection)

## 5836 (GHA 336D)

Wearing the NBC white coach livery, Plaxton Panorama C36F-bodied Leyland Leopard PSU3/4R 5836 (GHA 336D) has turned out of Mill Lane having just left Digbeth coach station, Birmingham. It had entered service in July 1966 and was classified as an LC9. It was re-seated to C40F in February 1973. The rather brash body styling of the Plaxton bodywork, the usually unpleasantly anonymous all-over white livery did subdue the worst excess of the embellishments on the coach's panelling. 5836 was converted to a recovery vehicle and painted into the overall yellow ancillary fleet livery, using the trade plate 067 HA. It re-entered service in October 1978 and lasted until it was finally withdrawn in January 2002. (Travel Lens)

## 6141 (SHA 641G)

Not every day trip was blessed with good weather. Here the first of the fifteen LC10 Plaxton-bodied Leyland Leopard PSU4A/4Rs, 6146 (SHA 641G), is parked at Oxford services on a really unpleasant day when on its way back from Portsmouth. 6141 was new in May 1969 and spent most of its early life at Leamington garage. After quite a short service life of only seven years, it was sold in February 1977 to Cumberland Motor Services. (D. R. Harvey Collection)

## 6147 (SHA 647G)

Working on a Scottish tour, 6147 (SHA 647G) was a Leyland Leopard PSU4A/4R that was equipped with the larger Leyland 11.1-litre 0680 engine. They had the clean-lined, rather tasteful Plaxton-designed Panorama Elite C36C bodies and these luxurious touring coaches weighed in at a solid 7 tonnes 17 cwt. Noteworthy is the location of the offside emergency door immediately behind the driver's seat. They were classified LC10 by Midland Red. 6147 is parked in High Street, Moffat, Dumfriesshire, on 19 July 1970. Behind it is the AA Two Star Balmoral Hotel, an eighteenth-century former coaching inn. Next door to the hotel is a shop selling Scottish souvenirs and tartan woollen goods in a town which historically was at the centre of the Scottish Georgian wool industry. (A. J. Douglas)

## 6149 (SHA 649G)

The 6141–6155 batch, classified LC10 by Midland Red, were designed specifically for excursion and tours. 6149, SHA 649G, is being employed on one such Scottish tour which were for 7, 9, 10 or 12 days in duration. The fully inclusive fare covered accommodation in first class hotels, meals at the hotel and en route gratuities. 6149 was a Leyland Leopard PSU4A/4R and had Plaxton Panorama Elite C36C body. It is parked at the ferry terminal at Fort William alongside Loch Linnhe on 13 June 1972. (A. J. Douglas)

## 6236 (WHA 236H)

Crossing the boundary from Birmingham into Sutton Coldfield in Sutton Road, Erdington, is 6236 (WHA 236H). Classified as the LC11 by Midland Red, the coaches were similar to the earlier LC9 batch but without the aluminium brightwork around the front of the coachwork. 6236 was a 36-foot-long Leyland Leopard PSU3A/4R with a Plaxton Panorama Mk I body with C49F seating capacity. This rather enhanced their appearance as it made them look less flash and more sober and dependable, which was more attuned to the traditional image being put forward by Midland Red. These coaches had the powerful Leyland 0.680 11.1-litre engine coupled to a pneumocyclic gearbox, which made the coaches far more driver-friendly, though they were not fitted with power steering. It is painted in the corporate NBC all-over-white livery which quickly became grubby. The overall effect was not helped by the garishly large 'NATIONAL' lettering with only a reluctant nod to who actually owned the coach. (Travel Lens)

## 6247 (WHA 247H)

The bodywork on these Leyland Leopards was Plaxton's Panorama type which was similar to the LC9s 5824–5838 but without the flashy corrugated aluminium ribbing at the front of the body. This more restrained style accentuated the large saloon windows from which the model name Panorama was derived. 6247 (WHA 247H) turns out of Edgbaston Street into Pershore Street when still retaining the patina of a brand-new coach. Behind it is the 1947-built S&U furniture store, which in later years transformed their goods-based credit businesses into a finance and HP operation. Owned by the Coombs family, who owned Birmingham City FC, the store manager for many years was the Blues goalkeeper Gil Merrick, who got twenty-three caps for England, though one of these was when England were beaten for the first time ever at Wembley when Merrick picked the ball out of his net six times! (A. J. Douglas)

## 6248 (WHA 248H)

Parked near to the railway station in Aberystwyth, on 11 September 1971, is 6248 (WHA 248H). New in July 1970, and initially allocated to Kidderminster garage, this 36-foot-long Plaxton C49F-bodied Leyland Leopard PSU3A/4R briefly moved to Midland Red (East) Ltd, Leicester, for the last ten months of its service life, before being withdrawn in April 1983. But here, twelve years earlier, 6248, with a maroon-coloured roof and chromed hub-caps, looks in fine fettle. (D. R. Harvey Collection)

## 6256 (6170 WJ)

In June 1970 Midland Red purchased five second-hand Leyland Leopard L1s with Weymann Fanfare C41F bodies. They were all new into the Sheffield C fleet in July 1960 and were repainted and fitted for one-man operation. They were allocated to Sheepcote Street garage, Birmingham. Although built as coaches, the coach was never used in that capacity, being used for bus work on the routes between Birmingham and Coleshill. They had a very short career with Midland Red, barely being in service for twelve months. 6256 (6170 WJ), formerly Sheffield 1170, was painted in an all-over red livery as one of the batch numbered 6256–6260, which somehow always looked drab and unloved. It is working on the 161 route and is turning into Lower Temple Street from Corporation Street. It is picking up passengers outside the premises of H. P. Pope, who were a high-class stationer, the premises being known as Pope's Corner. This was one of the longest lived of these five buses but even so it was taken out of service in July 1971. It does seem strange that these five vehicles were bought at all. As they were never given a Midland Red type number it suggests that they were never intended for use as a coach and sold to Hulley's of Baslow, Derbyshire. (D. R. Harvey Collection)

## 6447 (AHA 447J)

The last coaches purchased by Midland Red to receive fleet numbers in the original series were fifteen coaches designated C12 by the company. They were numbered 6446–6460. The second eof the batch, 6447 (AHA 447J), a Leyland Leopard PSU4B/4R Plaxton Panorama Elite II with C40F bodywork, stands in the then bus station in Rigby Road, Blackpool, in company with 1252 HE – an earlier Leyland Leopard, with a Plaxton body, owned by Yorkshire Traction. The weather looks autumnal and it could well be that the driver might have to do what nearly all coach drivers to Blackpool in the autumn months dreaded, namely 'the lights', which inevitably meant a return to the garage in the wee small hours! (D. R. Harvey Collection)

## 6450 (AHA 450J)

6450 (AHA 450J), a Leyland Leopard PSU4B/4R Plaxton Panorama Elite II with C40F bodywork is parked at the Caerthillian, near Helston, on the Lizard Peninsula, in the summer of 1971. The nearby Caerthillian Cove is a rocky inlet with a sandy beach near to Lizard Point and is a location known today for surfing; in the early 1970s it was better known to bird watchers. The coach is on one of Midland Red's coach cruises which were of either of seven or ten days' duration. 6450 entered service in May 1971 and was written-off after an accident in June 1981. (D. R. Harvey Collection)

## 6451 (AHA 451J)

Parked in the Aston Villa FC car park alongside the now sadly closed Aston Manor Museum, on 16 October 2011, is the preserved Plaxton Panorama Elite II-bodied Leyland Leopard PSU4B/4R 6451 (AHA 451J). New in May 1971, this forty-seat coach was allocated to no less than seven different Midland Red garages during its twelve years in their ownership. It was subsequently sold to Confidence Coaches of Oadby, who operated it for another fourteen years before it was purchased in June 1997 for preservation. It is now part of the Wythall Transport Museum's collection. (D. R. Harvey)

## 6455 (CHA 455K)

The last seven of the 1971 batch of Plaxton C40F-bodied Leyland Leopard PSU4B/4Rs were delivered in December 1971, some five months after the changeover from the suffix letters J to K. 6455 (CHA 455K) passes through a sunny Doncaster when empty but between passenger carrying duties during a Scottish tour. It is looking very smart, which was unusual for the all-over white NBC coach livery as it deteriorated in its appearance within about a year from its last repaint. In the recession period of the early 1970s, it was very difficult for operators to keep their vehicles looking smart, but in this case Midland Red had succeeded. Alas, after sale in 1981, it was severely damaged by a fire during the following year and immediately was scrapped. (R. F. Mack)

# The New Fleet
# Numbering System

In October 1972, Midland Red received the first of its Leyland National Mk Is and it was an appropriate time for the fleet numbering system to start with a more significant number. This first bus had the fleet number 101 and by October 1972 the first coach was delivered as 179 in this new series. There were 156 Leyland Leopards delivered in the new series with all but thirty having some variant of the Plaxton-built Panorama Elite or Supreme body. The remaining thirty Leopards had Willowbrook bodywork, one of which had the distinction of being numbered 844 which was the highest fleet number in this series. Finally, there was a solitary Leyland Tiger chassis, also bodied by Plaxton, which but for the split-up of the company in September 1981 might have become the new standard vehicle for Midland Red Coaches. But it was not to be!

## 186 (HHA 186L)

Looking a little less than pristine, a half full 186 (HHA 186L) leaves Cheltenham bus station on a somewhat indistinctly indicated destination. This Leyland Leopard PSU4B/4R had a Plaxton Panorama Elite III C40F body and was delivered to Midland Red in February 1973. After nearly ten years' service 186 was sold to Yardley's Coaches of Birmingham, who ran it for another nine years before it was stripped by them and sold to Birds Commercial Motors (dealer), at Long Marston, in December 1993, for scrap. (D. R. Harvey Collection)

## 196 (HHA 196L)

Travelling through the centre of Derby on 14 October 1983 is 196 (HHA 196L), wearing the local Chaserider branding of Midland Express. This was one of the eight coaches numbered 191–198 and designated C13 by Midland Red. It was a Leyland Leopard PSU3B/4R and had a Plaxton Panorama Elite III bodywork and had a reduced C44F seating capacity. It was originally delivered in the NBC overall white coach livery. It is working on the X60 express stage carriage service to Nottingham from Ironbridge via Telford, Wolverhampton, Cannock, Lichfield and Derby when it was allocated to Cannock garage. (D. R. Harvey Collection)

## 300 (PHA 300M)

Another twenty Plaxton Panorama Elite III-bodied Leyland Leopard PSU3E/4RTs were delivered between April and May 1974, each had a ten-speed pneumocyclic gearboxes. The batch, given the type code C14, was numbered 299–318 and all had a C44FT layout with the nearside rear toilet making them suitable for long-distance motorway coach work. In the all-over white National Bus Company livery, these coaches largely replaced the BMMO CM6T motorway coaches. The second member of the class, 300 (PHA 300M), is parked in Victoria coach station in London during November 1977. (C. W. Routh)

### 313 (PHA 313M)

Whereas the section of Pool Meadow bus station used by Coventry Corporation's municipal buses was two long rows of bus shelters and well-made road service, on the other side of the entrance road, off Fairfax Street, was the far more basic area used by Midland Red for both its express coach services and their stage carriage routes. A bus and coach station have occupied the site since 1931 but the eastern half was only given proper facilities in 1994. 313 (PHA 313M), a Panorama Elite III-bodied Leyland Leopard PSU3E/4RT is about to leave Pool Meadow on the Coventry to London motorway express 501 service. By now, the NBC had introduced nationwide route numbers for all its long-distance scheduled coach routes. These twenty C14s were the final Plaxton Panorama Elite-bodied coaches purchased by Midland Red. (D. R. Harvey Collection)

### 446 (JOX 446P)

About to leave the Red Lion bus station at Bridgefoot, in Stratford-upon-Avon, is 446 (JOX 446P). Opposite the bus station was the former garage premises of Stratford Blue Motors. On 4 September 1977, when the coach was barely eighteen months old and was still in the all-over white livery of Midland Red's corporate NBC owners, the coach appears to have only one passenger. 446, one of the nine C15s, is allocated to Leamington garage where it remained for its first two years of its service life. This was sixth of nine Leyland Leopard PSU3C/4Rs and entered service in February 1976 from Digbeth garage. They were the first of a large number of coaches delivered with Plaxton Supreme bodywork with a C47F seating layout. (F. W. York)

## 449 (JOX 449P)

Leaving St Margaret's bus station in Leicester, in April 1986, just eight months before it was withdrawn, is 444 (JOX 444P) – a Leyland Leopard PSU3C/4R with a Plaxton Supreme C47F body. Purchased for coach work, it was new in March 1976 and was by now owned by Midland Red East with Midland Fox legal lettering. 444 is working on the X66 express service to Birmingham via the M69 and Coventry, which was timetabled to take two hours. (D. R. Harvey Collection)

## 451 (JOX 451P)

450–470 were Leyland Leopard PSU3C/4Rs but with this time with Plaxton Supreme Express C49F bodywork. They were built to the Labour Government's bus grant specification, with two-piece powered doors and extra handrails. These dual-purpose Leopards were a delight to drive as they had pneumocyclic gearboxes, a large 11.1-litre engine and power steering. Fitted for one-man operation from new, they were delivered in the rather smart-looking red and white NBC dual-purpose livery and were classified C16 by Midland Red. 451 (JOX 451P) has just left the Birmingham bus station in the subterranean depths of the Bull Ring Centre, on 31 January 1976, and is turning right into Dudley Street from Edgbaston Street. It is working on the X92 service to Ludlow via Halesowen, Kidderminster, Cleobury Mortimer and the fearsome climb over Clee Hill on a journey that took two hours and twenty minutes. (D. R. Harvey Collection)

## 458 (JOX 458P)

With the top of the Grand Theatre in Lichfield Street just visible above the ventilation duct on the roof of the Plaxton body, 458 (JOX 458P) has just turned into the newly opened Wolverhampton bus station that had been completed in 1986. On a bitterly cold day in early 1987, with snow still on the ground, this forty-nine-seat Leyland Leopard PSU3C/4R, dating from January 1976, is about to work on the X89 service to Birmingham when in Midland Red North's Tellus livery and allocated to Wellington garage. By July 1987, JOX 458P had entered service with Midland Red West at Hereford garage. (D. R. Harvey Collection)

## 462 (JOX 462P)

Pressed into long-distance work, 462 (JOX 462P) stands in Oxford bus service when operating on the long 929 express service to Poole. It is a Leyland Leopard PSU3C/4R with Plaxton Supreme Express C49F bodywork. New in June 1976, 462 came into Midland Red South ownership on 6 September 1981, when that company was formed after the split-up of the original Midland Red Company. It was repainted into the white, yellow and red NBC Midland Express livery in May 1983, and into the white National Express colours in February 1985. Thus 462 is being used at a point between those livery change dates. (D. R. Harvey)

## 614 (NOE 614R)

A further six Plaxton Supreme C47F-bodied Leyland Leopard PSU3D/4Rs, classified as C17s, were delivered between November 1976 and March 1977. Speeding along St Martin's Queensway, on its way to take up service from Birmingham's bus station from Digbeth garage, is Leyland Leopard PSU3D/4R 614 (NOE 614R). This Plaxton C47F-bodied coach was new in December 1976 as a C17-type. They were very similar to the earlier C15s and were also designed for coach work. In February 1985 it was fitted with a DAF engine. It was finally withdrawn from Digbeth garage in March 1991 and was eventually converted into a towing vehicle based at Worcester garage until the end of 2010. (D. R. Harvey)

## 665 (RDA 665R)

The long X6 route was operated by Redditch garage and operated between Birmingham and Evesham via Alvechurch, Redditch, Studley and Alcester. The journey took well over two and a half hours and once at the bus station in Evesham, which was little more than a lay-by in the high street with virtually no facilities, the driver, who on arrival in Evesham had to find a public toilet, had no option but to use a lavatory in one of the nearby public houses. Midland Red policy was that going into licensed premises was a dismissible offence and frequently there was an Evesham garage inspector ready to pounce! 665 (RDA 665R) was a Leyland Leopard PSU3E/4R with C49F Plaxton Supreme Express bodywork and was new in July 1977 as type C18. This was the first of eighteen delivered in red and white NBC DP livery and built to bus grant specification with two-piece doors, extra handrails and fitted for one-man operation from new. With their power steering these dual-purpose vehicles were a delight to drive. It was finally withdrawn in August 1995. (D. R. Harvey Collection)

## 671 (SOA 671S)

On 26 November 1986, 671 (SOA 671S), a bus grant pattern Plaxton C49F-bodied Leyland Leopard PSU3E/4R owned by Midland Red West, stands in Halesowen bus station outside the Cornbow shopping centre that had been built in 1967. It is about to set off for Bromsgrove via the stiff climb to Romsley on the 335 service. This journey of barely ten miles took thirty-seven minutes. This service was given up in 1991 and the local independent operator, Ludlow's of Halesowen, took it over until the company was bought by the Rotala Group in April 2008. 671 passed to Midland Red West in 1981 and by now had been in the yellow and red Midland Express livery for over eighteen months. Behind the single-decker is 2915 (D915 NDA), a Travel West Midlands MCW Metrobus II in Timesaver livery with coach seats and a five-speed gearbox used for limited stop services. In this case it is working on the 900 service from Halesowen to Birmingham, Birmingham International Airport and Coventry. (D. R. Harvey)

## 728 (WOC 728T)

Parked in Manchester, having just worked on the 806 service, and looking a bit mud splattered is 728 (WOC 728T). New in November 1978, this Leyland Leopard PSU3E/4R, with Plaxton Supreme C46F bodywork as type code C19, was initially allocated to Digbeth garage for long-distance coach work. It is wearing the NBC national white coach livery with local MIDLAND RED fleet names on the front flank. The Plaxton bodies were so designed that they could be used for coach work as well as the longer stage carriage services. 728 was finally withdrawn in May 1985. (D. R. Harvey Collection)

## 736 (WOC 736T)

Parked outside Tamworth garage wearing Midland Red North's Mercian livery is 736 (WOC 736T). This was one of the twelve Leyland Leopard PSU3E/4Rs that were classified C20 by Midland Red and that had entered service in April 1979. It was delivered in the red and white NBC dual-purpose livery and had been built to bus grant specification with two-piece doors. It was equipped for one-man operation with electric power points for the ticket machine. The Plaxton C49F body had been repainted in June 1985 into red strip Mercian bus livery. Opened on 3 August 1928, Aldergate garage had an allocation of about forty-four vehicles including coach-bodied Leyland Leopards such as 736. (D. R. Harvey Collection)

## 741 (WOC 741T)

741 (WOC 741T) was the last of the twelve Leyland Leopard PSU3E/4Rs, with Plaxton Supreme Express C49F bodywork, to be delivered. New in May 1979 as type C20, it is working on the X96 route opposite the Georgian Tontine Hotel and alongside the entrance the world-famous Ironbridge. Abraham Darby III built the cast iron bridge and the 100-foot-long bridge was opened on New Year's Day 1781. It was built in order to cross the River Severn, about 50 feet above the normal level of the river, at a point where it flowed through a quite narrow gorge. The gorge carries the River Severn south towards the Bristol Channel. It formed during the last part of the Pleistocene ice age when the water from the previously north-flowing pre-present day River Dee became trapped in Lake Lapworth, which was created when the Irish Sea ice sheet dammed the river. The lake level rose until the water overflowed through the hills to the south. This flow eroded a path through the hills, forming the gorge and permanently diverting the Severn southwards. 741 stands at the bus stop in Tontine Hill, Ironbridge, alongside the war memorial in the local Hotspur livery. (Dorset Transport Circle)

## 777 (BVP 777V)

Standing in the small coach parking area, alongside the entrance to Digbeth coach station, adjacent to Rea Street, in April 1987, are 777 (BVP 777V) and 775 (BVP 775V) – two of the ten Leyland Leopard PSU3E/Rs classified as C21 by Midland Red. These had Plaxton Supreme IV bodywork C53F from new and were purchased for use as long-distance coaches. 777 entered service in January 1980 from Digbeth garage and passed to Midland Red Express on the breakup of the original company, on 6 September 1981. By March 1985 it had been repainted into the Midland Red Coaches livery (the livery it is wearing) as does the identical coach 775, BVP 775V, parked alongside. (D. R. Harvey)

## 780 (BVP 780V)

Wearing the original all-over white national coach livery is 780 (BVP 780V), a Plaxton Supreme IV C53F-bodied Leyland Leopard PSU3E/R classified as a C21-type. It is passing the front of Windsor Castle in Thames Street, during 1981, when operating on an excursion from Birmingham. Many of the passengers are looking towards the castle but Her Majesty was not in! The coach entered service in January 1980 and was converted to a one-man operation dual-purpose vehicle by Midland Red East in October 1984. (D. R. Harvey Collection)

## 784 (BVP 784V)

The Midland Red type CDP23s consisted of a batch of five Leyland Leopard PSU3E/4R coaches, numbered 784–788. These were new in June and July 1980 and fitted with C53F Plaxton Supreme IV Express bodywork built to bus grant specification with two-piece jackknife bus doors. Whilst on loan to Midland Red Express, Birmingham, in September 1981, 784 (BVP 784V) was used on a private hire trip to Crich Tramway Museum. It is painted in the white, red and yellow livery and stands in front of the Derby Assembly Rooms façade. 784 remained in service until eventually being withdrawn by Arriva Midlands North in November 1998. (D. R. Harvey)

## 795 (BVP 795V)

Speeding along Newtown Row in Birmingham, when operating on the X31 route during October 1984, is 795 (BVP 795V). This single-decker was a Leyland Leopard PSU3E/4R with Willowbrook 003 Express C53F bodywork, which was built to bus grant specification with two-piece doors, extra handrails and equipped for one-man operation. There were eighteen of these dual-purpose coaches acquired by Midland Red, numbered 789–806, and 795 (BVP 795V) entered service in June 1980 classified by Midland Red as a CDP22. It spent its entire service life based at Cannock garage. Early in its career it was repainted in this white, yellow and red NBC Midland Express livery. 795, like all these Willowbrook-bodied vehicles, was very short lived due to the generally poor body construction. In this case it was withdrawn in April 1987. (D. R. Harvey)

### 799 (BVP 799V)

22 September 1981 was a wet and miserable day, as the poorly patronised 799 (BVP 799V) turns out of the coach part of Pool Meadow bus station, in Coventry, when working on the X67 service to Stratford-upon-Avon. The X67 route took exactly one hour to get from Coventry to Stratford via Leamington Spa and Warwick. 799, a Leyland Leopard PSU3E/4R with Willowbrook 003 Express C53F bodywork, in the smart red and white dual-purpose livery of the NBC was barely fourteen months old. 799 was allocated for most of its life to Leicester Southgate Street garage and was finally withdrawn in January 1991. (D. R. Harvey Collection)

### 806 (BVP 806V)

The driver collects the last passenger's fare prior to leaving the Parade in Sutton Coldfield in 806 (BVP 806V). This dual-purpose coach is a rather mud-bespattered Leyland Leopard PSU3E/4R with Willowbrook 003 Express C53F bodywork. It had been delivered to Midland Red during September 1980. 806 is being used on the long X99 express service from Birmingham to Nottingham by way of Tamworth (its next stop) and Ashby-de-la-Zouch, on a journey that would have taken two hours forty-five minutes and had fifteen services every weekday. (D. R. Harvey)

## 832 (LOA 832X)

New with a C51F Plaxton Supreme IV body, 832 (LOA 832X) was the only Leyland Tiger to be purchased by the Midland Red Omnibus Company and entered service on 20 September 1981. 832 had the distinction of being the last vehicle to be acquired by Midland Red before the parent company was closed and split up in September 1981 and was given the Midland Red code C25. 832 is parked alongside the Rea Street entrance to Digbeth coach station, in Birmingham, and is painted in the National Holidays livery of Midland Red coaches. 832 was the TRCTL11/3R version of the new Tiger model, which succeeded the long-lived Leopard types in 1981, and was a totally new mid-engined chassis with full air suspension and the TL11 11.1-litre underfloor engine. 832 would eventually pass to Western National Ltd, in Truro, in June 1997, and was withdrawn from service in January 1998. (D. R. Harvey Collection)

## 836 (LOA 836X)

A further twelve Willowbrook 003 Express-bodied Leyland Leopard PSU3F/4R chassis numbered 833–844 were delivered to MROC in 1980 but then placed in store until 1982. The Willowbrook 003 bodies were not particularly well constructed and required a considerable amount of remedial work during their lifetime. For example, immediately after delivery, they spent a considerable amount of time in Carlyle Road Works's body shop with panels removed and frames being refabricated. The design of the body took elements of the Duple Dominant coach body and a certain resemblance at the front to the contemporary ECW coach model, but the overall effect just didn't look right. They were built to bus grant specification with two-piece doors for use on limited stop stage services. Built to a C53F layout, within a year this was reduced to a lower C49F seating capacity. 836 entered service in June 1982 and is parked in Pool Meadow's coach park, in Coventry, having renumbered 536 in January 1983. (D. R. Harvey Collection)